CITY OF LIONS

Amy Byrd

LifeWay Press® Nashville, Tennessee

STUDENT MINISTRY
PUBLISHING

Ben Trueblood
Director, Student Ministry

John Paul Basham
*Manager, Student
Ministry Publishing*

Karen Daniel
Editorial Team Leader

Morgan Hawk
Content Editor

Jennifer Siao
Production Editor

Sarah Nikolai
Graphic Designer

© 2018 LifeWay Press®

Requests for permission should be addressed in writing to LifeWay Press®, One LifeWay Plaza, Nashville, TN 37234.

ISBN: 978-1-4627-9229-0
Item Number: 005801327

Dewey Decimal Classification Number: 248.83
Subject Heading: RELIGION / Christian Ministry / Youth

Printed in the United States of America.

We believe that the Bible has God for its author; salvation for its end; and truth, without any mixture of error, for its matter and that all Scripture is totally true and trustworthy. To review LifeWay's doctrinal guideline, please visit www.lifeway.com/doctrinalguideline.

Unless otherwise noted, all Scripture quotations are taken from the Christian Standard Bible®, Copyright © 2017 by Holman Bible Publishers. Used by permission. Christian Standard Bible® and CSB® are federally registered trademarks of Holman Bible Publishers.

Scripture quotations marked (ESV) are from the ESV® Bible (The Holy Bible, English Standard Version®), copyright © 2001 by Crossway, a publishing ministry of Good News Publishers. Used by permission. All rights reserved.

Student Ministry Publishing
LifeWay Resources
One LifeWay Plaza
Nashville, TN 37234

table of contents

about the author

Amy Byrd has a desire to make much of Jesus and loves all things student ministry. She has the joy of serving as the Director of Girls Ministry at Hunter Street Baptist Church in Birmingham, Alabama. Amy is also the author of *Worthy Vessel* and co-author of *Dwell*. Her ultimate desire is to see girls know their worth as daughters of the Most High and know Him as their Savior. She's the mom of a handsome little boy, Timothy, and the wife of a hard-working husband. She loves working in her garden and eating chips and salsa. You can connect with Amy on Instagram at amy_byrd.

a note from Amy

Friend,

It is a privilege to meet you here on these pages. I do not know your story. Where you have been. What you have gone through. You do not know my story. (However, you will learn more about me in the pages ahead than you may like to know.)

What I do know is we have a King who was intentional in bringing us together to study the Book of Daniel. I am praying the God who saved my life and continues to transform me from the inside out will do the same for you.

He is strength. He is wisdom. He is perfect. He is good. He is the one true King. And He loves you. And I love you too.

I cannot wait to see where He takes us in the next few weeks.

Big Group Hug!

Amy

how to use

In this book, you will find seven weeks of group sessions and six weeks of personal study. We encourage you to work through the personal study at your own pace, and it can all be completed in an afternoon or over the span of four days. As you begin your group time, watch the video to hear from the heart of the author and get a quick introduction to the session's passage of Scripture. There is also a leader guide included in the back of this study with helpful tips to use during group time. Once girls have completed this study, they will have completed a timeline of Daniel's faith journey and learned what it looks like to stand with faith and integrity in the midst of opposition.

BIBLE STUDY BOOK

Listed below are the different elements in the Bible study book.

Group Discussion

Questions and cultural connections are provided to help guide the conversation.

Personal Study

Personal Bible study which can be done at your own pace will help reinforce the theme and provide an opportunity to dig deeper into the Scripture.

Leader Guide

The leader guide at the back of the study provides ideas for activities and deeper group discussions.

SESSION OUTLINE

Design your group sessions to fit the space, time, and needs of your girls. The following is a sample group session outline you can adapt.

1. Press Play.

Review the material in the previous week's personal Bible study and watch the video.

2. Let's Talk.

Scripture and discussion questions are provided to help foster conversation among the group.

3. Here & Now.

Answer the final questions together and spend some time comparing Babylon to today's culture. Close the session with prayer.

Daniel's timeline

605 BC

(605–562 BC)
Nebuchadnezzar is king of Babylon

First Babylonian invasion of Judah—Daniel and other princes taken into captivity in Babylon

Daniel's ministry begins

573 BC

Nebuchadnezzar's dream of a tree

562 BC

Nebuchadnezzar dies

572 BC

Nebuchadnezzar's seven years of insanity

603–

602 BC

Nebuchadnezzar's
dream of a statue

Shadrach, Meshach,
and Abednego thrown
into the furnace

552 BC

(552–539 BC)
Belshazzar is king
of Babylon

539 BC

Handwriting on the wall

Belshazzar dies

Babylon falls to Persia

Darius the Mede made king

536 BC

Daniel thrown
into lions' den
(88 years old)

set
apart

Daniel _____ that he would not defile himself with the king's food or with the wine he drank. **Daniel 1:8**

Have there been moments in your world that the culture has influenced you to do something? Explain.

What was the eunuch's response to Daniel's request to eat something different?

Why was Daniel able to have confidence in being tested?

What was the result of the testing after 10 days?

Does looking different scare you?

Looking different is _____.

Looking different is _____.

We're not supposed to look like everybody else because we're modeling our lives after _____.

Use the space provided to note any Scripture references or comments from the video you want to remember.

let's talk

We live in a world of much. A world of more. A world of me, me, me. Every day we are bombarded with voices telling us how to look great, get smart, make more, and be the best at what we do. Before our eyes are magazines and TV shows with celebrities' lives featured and celebrated because of the money in their bank accounts, their dress sizes, or the number of followers they have on social media.

Think about it for a minute. Step outside of what you know to be normal and really consider the world around you. What images come to mind when you think about our culture? What do you consider to be the theme of life in general? What is our focus? Our priority?

In what ways does culture shape your life?

That question sounds kind of big, but really, what do you do simply because you have seen celebrities or people in magazines doing it? What do you wear because you've seen "everyone at school" wearing it? (I'll tell you a funny story about that later.)

Whether we notice it or not, culture shapes us! It influences everyone in one way or another. And it may be shaping us in some ugly and dark ways that we don't see. Pride grows deep in us like ivy. Selfishness and sin abound. We run ourselves ragged trying to keep up with the latest trends and be "in" enough so that we don't look odd. And here we find ourselves. You and me. Smack-dab in the middle of a world that influences us every day, and most of the time we don't even notice.

You need to know that I am a normal gal. My "fancy" days often hit their peak with some sassy shoes, a quiet trip to Target, and a Diet Coke the size of my face. I usually only wear my crown on Thursdays—but that kind of depends on the weather. Are you paying attention? No crown 'round here. Just lots of bobby pins and dry shampoo.

I'm going to be honest and let you know that keeping up with our world overwhelms me. From politics to pumpkin protein smoothies, I can never seem to fully grasp the most up-to-date information or keep up with the latest trends. It isn't that I don't like Twitter or know how to work Instagram, it's more that I have learned over time that there is no point in trying to keep up. There is no value in the chase of being in the now—because by the time I catch up to the now I am late. No amount of blonde balayage or likes on my posts are ever going to satisfy me, because I cannot be satisfied by the things of the world. I was made for a different place—a place so different from our culture. It is perfect and holy and forever, while our culture is broken, vulgar, and temporary. And yet here the Lord has placed me. And you.

This seems like the proper time to introduce you to the book of the Bible we are setting up camp in for the next seven weeks. The Book of Daniel. A true story of a young man and his companions who were taken far from home and placed in the middle of a flashy culture, filled with sin. But before we learn more about Daniel himself, let's get a better picture of where he was living when we meet in chapter one.

Babylon was a visual beauty. Think fancy. Think extravagant. Think over the top. We are meeting these Babylonians in a time when their lives were built around having the best, surrounded by luxury and beauty. But they were empty. Take a moment to think about your ultimate picture of luxury.

What do you envision?

Some of us will see a penthouse overlooking Central Park. Others will imagine a giant cabin in the mountains. For me, it is a beautiful home at the beach. We all love beautiful things. If we're honest, we would all love to live a life of luxury. I mean, who wouldn't?

Our study begins in 605 BC when the empire had just conquered Jerusalem. At this time Babylon was ruled by King Nebuchadnezzar. You read that name right. Can we all agree that life is too short to say that name too many times? Let's just call him King Neb.

Take a moment to read Daniel 1:3-5.

In this passage, we see King Neb instruct one of his men to gather a group of children with specific gifts.

1. What qualities and traits did the king require?

2. What do these requests tell us about the king and his priorities?

3. Does this particular list remind you of scenarios you might find yourself in? School tryouts? Being asked to homecoming?

The king and his men wanted those who would serve them to look, act, and think in very specific ways. They were being brainwashed to look just alike. They were being trained by their culture to be people they were not. These boys were even required to change their names. This was a big factor in brainwashing them to become a part of the king's men. The purpose was to tie these men to local gods and deny the God of their past. Daniel means "God is my judge," but his name was changed to Belteshazzar meaning "Bel Protect the King."

Let's meet the other guys:

Given Name	Babylonian Name
Hananiah "God Has Been Gracious"	**Shadrach** "Command of Akku"
Mishael "Who Is What God Is?"	**Meshach** "Who Is What Aku Is?
Azariah "The Lord Has Helped"	**Abednego** "Servant of Nebo" [1]

FAST FACT: The Book of Daniel is named after and indicated to be written by the prophet Daniel, who wrote in the autobiographical first person beginning in chapter 7 verse 2 and throughout the rest of the book.[2]

Babylon was not Daniel's home and King Neb was not his true king. Daniel wasn't born in Babylon. Daniel was born into a wealthy family in Judah. He had a home. A life. And all of that changed the day he was taken to Babylon for the purpose of being trained by Babylonian leaders to deal with Jews who were being brought into the city. This young man was taken from his home where he was comfortable and safe, and planted into the middle of a turbulent and sinful empire. Can you imagine how terrifying that must have been? To be surrounded by a king and leaders who were telling you what to believe, who to be, and even what you must eat? Look back at Daniel 1:5 to see what the king instructed these young men to be fed.

With insight from his God, Daniel knew eating and drinking the delicacies King Neb had commanded was only for sinful purposes and not for their good. In faithful boldness, Daniel suggested a new plan.

Read Daniel 1:8-14 aloud.

What was the plan Daniel came up with for Shadrach, Meshach, Abednego, and himself?

Daniel was instructed to do something by King Neb, who essentially "owned" him, but rather than doing as he was told, he was obedient to God and suggested a different plan. That's what I like to call a bold move.

Could he have just done as he was told? Sure. Would the world have ended if Daniel had eaten some cake? Nope. But this is where his story gets life-changing. This will be our landing place for the entire study.

This is the only time I will encourage you to skip ahead in Daniel. Turn in your Bibles to Daniel 2:28 and circle it: "There is a God in heaven." The Creator of heaven and earth. Daniel's true King. Our true King. And Daniel only answered to Him. This gives us a glimpse of Daniel's obedience to the Lord and his trust in God's perfect plan for his life.

Try to put yourself in Daniel's place. I doubt you will ever have to say no to cake for the sake of honoring Jesus, but there will be moments in our lives when we are asked to do things we know do not honor Jesus. Cheat on a test. Lie to a friend. Sit among gossip. Go too far with a boy. Drugs. Alcohol. The possibilities are endless. And you might find yourself surrounded by a sea of people who are asking you to do something that you know you should not do. Will you be brave enough to speak up?

> Have you ever had a moment in your life when you had to make a bold move to choose Christ over our culture? Explain.

Daniel didn't give in. For ten days, Daniel and his friends drank only water and ate only vegetables. (Not my kind of diet, but I am proud of them. I would have requested ten days of Diet Coke and chips with salsa, but that's just me. Normal gal, remember?)

Let's dig into the rest of this passage and see how Daniel's plan played out.

Read Daniel 1:15-21.

> How did Daniel and his friends differ from the other young men?

> What does the passage say God gave them during these days?

Girls, my heart bursts reading the words in this passage of Scripture. It wasn't about the food. It wasn't about the calories. It was about not giving in. Not giving up. It was about the strength to not sink in and be like everyone else, but instead to be bold and different.

Daniel and his friends knew God had called them to be different and He honored them for their obedience.

I love what verses 19-20 say about the king's interview with the young men. Help me finish the passage:

> The king interviewed them, and among all of them, _____ _____ _____ _____ equal to _____, _____, _____, and _____. So they began to attend the king. In every matter of wisdom and understanding that the king consulted them about, he found them _____ _____ _____ than all the magicians and mediums in his entire kingdom.

Because these four men were so great? Nope. Because of their mighty God.

HERE & NOW

Remember when I said I would tell you a funny story?

When I was in seventh grade, I had a dream that I walked into school one morning and was surrounded by a sea of pink and purple North Face jackets. Picture this with me, people. Everywhere my 12-year-old eyes could see was a girl wearing the jacket. And I, without a jacket, felt like an outcast. No North Face. What a nightmare! Or so my middle school heart thought. This dream didn't come out of nowhere. That was the year that "every girl" got this particular jacket for Christmas, and I just missed the mark completely. Not only did I not ask for the jacket, I didn't even know it existed until Christmas break was over and everyone showed up to school in their fancy new outerwear! I felt like an outsider. A no-North-Face loser. Different from everyone else.

Now I want to ease your minds and let you know I did survive this outerwear trial. Though it was a close one. The reality is that, while this story is silly, I felt like an outsider because I didn't look like everyone else. I so longed to be like the rest of the girls in my grade. To keep up with the trends. To blend into the crowd and look the same. Certainly I am not alone in this. I believe that in our heart of hearts we can all acknowledge a time and a place in our lives when we have felt uncomfortably different.

But here's the thing—you were created to be different. There is a God in heaven who created you to be His. He created you to look like Him. He created you for another home. Yes, we are here in this time surrounded by Birchboxes, selfies, and boutiques galore—and we are allowed to be a part of these things. But we were created for much more. Just like Daniel, though we are far from our true home, we can be faithful to our purpose to serve our mighty God in the midst of a city of lions.

In your personal study this week, we are going to dive even deeper into this particular passage of Scripture. Girls, if you will dive in with me I promise you will see things in the midst of God's Word that will rock your world in the very best ways. His Word is active! His Word transforms! And I don't know about you, but my heart never gets enough time spent with Jesus.

Let's do this. Together.

Finish up your group time today discussing your answers to these questions:

Is it possible to be immersed in culture and not be influenced by it? Why or why not?

In what ways can you protect your heart from being consumed by culture?

Are you willing to look different from everyone else in order to honor Jesus? Explain.

List some specific ways this may play out in your own life.

How does biblical community and surrounding ourselves with believers help us in our battle against a hostile culture?

personal study

Hey you!

I'm gonna be really honest. I feel like most of you dread the "homework" portion of these studies that we get to do together. I get it. You just finished your chemistry, government, and AP English, and you have no desire to dive into *more* homework. So let's call it personal study.

We are going to make a deal. I will promise you that your personal study will be exciting and that you will actually learn something, if you will promise me that you will commit and dig in each week.

Deal? Deal.

You have some options when it comes to how you want to handle your personal study week to week.

You can sit down and complete it all in one day or you can break it up into several days of study each week. Along the way I am building in natural breaks for those of you who want to break it up into several days of study, or shorter pauses for those of you who just need five minutes to get a cupcake and a latte. I am a girl who likes options—Can I get a witness?

My hope is that this time of personal study will give you a better picture of the Book of Daniel and will help you apply it to your own life. There will be moments when we learn more about the history of this book of the Bible, and moments when I give you an opportunity to work through some of the Scripture on your own.

Either way I am asking God, in His mighty power, to transform us as we seek Him in His Word.

So, let's go.

SECTION 1: FAR FROM HOME
Daniel 1:1-4

Where we live matters. Where we are from matters. For some of us those places are one and the same. For example, I live in Birmingham, Alabama, and I was born in Birmingham, Alabama. I serve on staff at my home church where I was raised, and I live just a few miles away from the house where I grew up. Growing up in my hometown has certainly shaped me into who I am today. My family. My church. My best friends. My high school. My husband who I met in first grade Sunday school. (Is that not the cutest thing you've ever heard?) My worldview has been shaped by the place I call home.

If I was uprooted tomorrow and placed in a totally different culture, it would be a shock. New people. New sounds. New sights. New cultural norms. New languages. New difficulties. I have experienced that in small doses as I have traveled around the world.

My favorite city in the world is London. The sounds of the city thrill me. The tea and scones make my heart sing. The markets and the museums are incredible. I love to visit for weeks at a time and always enjoy every second that I am on British soil, but in the back of my heart there is always an ache for home.

The very definition of *home* is: a place of origin.[3]

And the definition of *origin* is: the point at which something begins.[4]

So, where do you live? And where are you from?

How would you describe your home? How does home make you feel?

Let's dig deeper into Daniel's history.

⟶ **Read Daniel 1:1-4.**

Let's work out some of these details together.

King Neb besieged _____.

The king commanded that some of the people of Israel would be brought to _____.

Among them were _____, _____, _____ and _____.

So if we were to make Daniel and his friends answer the questions that we answered above, they would say:

Where do you live? *Babylon*

Where are you from? *Jerusalem/Judah*

Can you imagine your home being overtaken by a cruel king, and then being exiled to live in a different city far away from your family and friends? Far from the comforts of home. Far from all that you have known for your entire life. Exiled. To serve a king.

The good news, girls, is that Daniel knew that this earth, no matter the location we may find ourselves, was not his ultimate home, and it is not ours either. Daniel trusted his God in heaven and knew that he was created for a different, permanent home where he would spend eternity.

> For we do not have an enduring city here; instead, we seek the one to come. **Hebrews 13:14**

Daniel and his friends knew that their God would protect them no matter where they were, even in the midst of a crazy culture like Babylon. Because they were created for more. And their purpose, while away from their eternal home, was to boast of their God and honor Him all of their days.

So, sister. I asked you where you live. I asked you where you are from. Now, I must ask, do you know that no matter where your home may be today that you were created for more? A different home. A perfect, holy eternal home. A place where we will worship God and enjoy Him forever. As followers of Christ, we are promised a place there! Right alongside these noble men who lived faithfully in exile in Babylon, our eternal home awaits!

Have you asked the Holy Spirit to take up residence in your heart and prepare you for your eternal home? Explain.

I encourage you now to take stock of your heart. I don't know about you, but in the midst of our current culture and state of our world, *home* sounds really beautiful right now.

Listen to "This Is My Inheritance" by All Sons And Daughters (*Poets and Saints*, 2016), and maybe grab an ice cream or take a walk before we continue on in our personal study for this session.

SECTION 2: FAITHFULNESS & FOOD
Daniel 1:5-13

I mentioned that I loved visiting London. It holds a really special place in my heart. It also happens to be the place where I tasted one of the most disgusting things ever. Y'all, I don't want to be dramatic, but I thought my taste buds were going to shut down for life because of what I put them through.

One word: *Marmite*. This is a sticky brown food paste that some Brits spread on toast, pair with cheese, and so on. And, listen, if you are one of the people that loves Marmite, I am sorry but you are crazy and I need to feed you some Nutella. That is the only sticky brown food paste that I am interested in.

Now to get to my point.

In 2011, I was at a church in Highgate for a potluck lunch and found myself in a kitchen surrounded by 20 of my British friends all watching as I was fed an industrial size spoonful of Marmite. No toast. No cheese. Just me and Marmite. As I "ate" the sticky brown paste, I found myself baffled that I was standing in a room full of people who ate this food regularly. This food was a part of their culture. A part of their norm.

Food is used for way more than eating. In every culture, food is a centerpiece. People use foods as vessels of communicating love, thanks, sympathy, and celebration. In Daniel's day, food also communicated a lot about your beliefs. Jews had a very specific diet that they followed. So when King Neb commanded the men to eat and drink very specific foods, Daniel and his friends had to make some decisions.

> **FAST FACT:** Read more about the food restrictions of Jews in Leviticus 11:1-47 and Deuteronomy 14:3-20. This will help you get a better picture of the food that was deemed "unclean" by the Jews.

Let's work through this next passage together. I am going to give you a chance to write out the key parts as you read them. I will get you started.

Read Daniel 1:5-13.

Let me take a moment to remind you that Daniel was defying the command of a cruel king who had kidnapped him from his home and taken him prisoner in Babylon. The boldness and bravery Daniel showed in standing up to the king's command is a testimony of his trust in the God who he served. Clearly Daniel knew that eating the diet provided by the king was about way more than calories and being treated to the spoils of the kingdom. To eat this food was to assimilate to the culture of the kingdom. Daniel and his friends were avoiding the luxurious foods provided by the king as a way of protection. Protection from the temptation to get caught up in the luxury of the city that surrounded them.

> But Daniel purposed in his heart that he would not defile himself with the portion of the king's meat, nor with the wine which he drank. **Daniel 1:8 (KJV)**

Circle these words: "purposed in his heart."

To whom did Daniel's heart belong?

Daniel and his friends were unwilling to do anything that might come between them and their God. The one true God. Not the gods and idols that those in Babylon were worshiping. So they were bold and they took a stand. Daniel "purposed in his heart" not to break his commitment to God.

In our world and current culture, eating specific foods probably isn't going to be the way you are tempted and tested most often. But there are other areas of our lives that might look luxurious, enticing, and exciting, yet may defile us. The definition of *defile* is: to make unclean or impure.[5] I've also heard it defined as corrupting purity or perfection.

Let's have some real talk for a moment. Being invited to parties. Getting attention from boys. Being included in the popular group of girls. Getting noticed by the scout from that college team. Getting an invitation to a certain school club. Fitting into that super small size you've dreamed about for a year. Getting asked to prom by *him*. All of these things on the surface may be good. Enticing. Exciting.

But are these things going to be used by the enemy as vessels to corrupt the purity and perfection of our hearts? Will they make us more unclean? More impure? Are they simply a part of our culture, and assimilating to the culture makes us just like everyone else?

No, sister, you may not be offered a feast by a king in the middle of a metropolis city. But you are being tempted by the *same* enemy Daniel was in the *same* ways. With pretty things that seem innocent, but are really just trying to lure us into loving and looking like the world around us. And as we learned this week in our group time—we were made for more. A better place. Our true home.

> Where are the places that you are being defiled?

> What delicacies of today are tempting you?

Cling to Jesus. Trust Him to satisfy you. He is better than any fantasy or feast.

Pause here to take a break. Get some coffee, eat a snack, and meet me back here.

SECTION 3: LOOKING DIFFERENT
Daniel 1:15-20

We paused at a cliffhanger. What makes me smile often while reading Daniel is that it feels like a CW nighttime television drama. Mainly because King Neb threatens to kill a different person for a different thing every time we turn the page.

To summarize where we were yesterday: King Neb commanded that all of the young men in his keep be fed a specific, luxurious diet in order to assimilate these men to the culture of Babylon. Daniel, Shadrach, Meshach, and Abednego refused to eat the diet. Daniel spoke with the chief of the eunuchs and requested that he and his friends be tested for ten days by allowing them to eat a diet that was different from the rest of the men.

Let's dive back in.

> **Read Daniel 1:15-20 and answer the following:**

What was the result of the ten-day meal plan Daniel requested?

What did the Lord give in reward for the obedience of these men?

What did the king do in verses 19-20?

This is one of my favorite passages in the entire Book of Daniel. This is an incredible moment. Remember the men in the king's keep were being fed the best foods and served the best drinks. They were being spoiled and treated as royalty so they would become more dependent on the king and his kingdom. Daniel and his three friends were eating a bare bones diet. Vegetables and water.

It would seem to me that the men who were fed the fatter, richer diet would be the most satisfied and filled at the end of the ten days. But as we learned in our last segment, it was about much more than food. Daniel and his friends were unwilling to participate in anything that might tempt them to bend to the culture. They refused to defile themselves. And at the end of the ten days, these men looked better in appearance than all of the men who ate the king's food!

Not only did these men look different because they went against the norm and were obedient to Christ, but they also looked physically different from the other men as well! God rewarded Daniel and his friends for their obedience by giving them wisdom and understanding that far exceeded that of even the enchanters and magicians of the kingdom. Why? Because our God rewards those who obey Him.

Obedience to God will cause us to look different. Obedience to God will call us to do difficult things. Obedience to God will require taking risks.

SECTION 4: RESPOND

Friend, God's Word has called us to do a lot of self-examination this week. And that isn't going to stop anytime soon during this study. God's Word is alive and is transformational—meaning that it quite literally changes us. It changes our lives. It changes our days. It changes our details. And my prayer for you at this moment is that you might open your heart and ask God to use His Word to change you.

I do not know you. I do not know about your life. But I do know a God who knows and cares deeply about the details of your heart and your soul. I do know that God longs to have the affections of your whole heart. He desires that you would flee from the things that defile you and instead seek satisfaction in Him.

Will taking steps toward God change the way your life looks? Yes. 100 percent. Absolutely. Don't you think Daniel felt a little different when he refused to eat the food everyone else was eating?

You will look different. Because, God willing, you will *be* different.

I want you to end this week working through the chart below. This is your call to acknowledge and to act. We are going to end every week like this, so buckle up, buttercup—it's time to take the truth and put it into action.

List some ways your life either shows you are devoted to Christ or to our culture in the chart that follows.

Culture	Christ

After you finish, I want you to journal a prayer. Ask God to give you boldness to address all of the items listed under "culture" and to help you learn some tangible ways to surrender those things. Ask God to protect in mighty ways the areas of your heart and your life that are devoted to Him.

> **5** "He announced, 'Turn, each of you, from your evil way of life and from your evil deeds. Live in the land the LORD gave to you and your ancestors long ago and forever. **6** Do not follow other gods to serve them and to bow in worship to them, and do not anger me by the work of your hands. Then I will do you no harm.'" **7** "'But you have not obeyed me'—this is the LORD's declaration—'with the result that you have angered me by the work of your hands and brought disaster on yourselves.'" **Jeremiah 25:5-7**

My prayer is that the Lord begins a work in your heart this very moment that changes you. The weeks ahead are going to be rich in truth and hard in practice. Stay with me.

SESSION TWO

your people

What is the first thing King Nebuchadnezzar does after having his troubling dream?

What gives Daniel such confidence in his ability to interpret the dream?

What does Daniel do after asking the king for a chance to interpret his dream?

Our people are _____.

But there is a _____ in _____ who provides and who protects.

What was the king's response to Daniel's interpretation of the dream?

Use the space provided to note any Scripture references or comments from the video you want to remember.

let's talk

Session two! Welcome back. I am proud you returned. Consistency in our study is huge, and I am going to celebrate with you every time you meet me here. I promise our time digging into Scripture will be worth it.

I don't know about y'all but I spent a lot of last week noticing some little things about our culture I had paid attention to before. I noted every brand name shoe and Starbucks cup I passed. The sparkle and fancy of magazine covers and the filtered social media worlds of those who we follow—wow.

Last session, I asked you to consider the ways culture affects your life. The way you dress. Your social media posts. How you fix your hair. Whether we realize it or not, culture is shaping us in many ways. And, as we learned in our personal study, our culture often defiles our hearts.

This week is all about our people.

I, personally, love people. I gain energy from being surrounded by them. Yet at the same time, I find people quite exhausting. I like to think of myself as an introverted extrovert with a sprinkle of hermit.

We have different categories of people who we encounter. We have our family. They are our love-it-or-hate-it, in-good-and-in-bad, born-with-them kind of people. Family dynamics for each of us will be different, but we all, in some form or fashion, can identify with the family group.

We have our casual acquaintances. The people we pass in the hallway. The ones we always run into at Target. The ones whose names we know but whose details we don't.

And then, we have our *people*. No need for another word. They are *your people*. The ones who know you. That you can call at any time, day or night. The ones who can order you food basically anywhere because they know what you want. I have a very small handful of *people*. They know my heart. They know my tone. They know the details of my days. And they are very important to me.

I don't want to say anything else until I say this. What is coming next is going to step on some toes. It might make you uncomfortable or even hurt. Please know that my aim is not to create drama or cause pain. My job here isn't to tell you things that make you happy, but instead is to point you to Jesus. Hear my heart on that. Okay? Okay. Good talk.

Our people matter. They matter because we love them, yes. But they also matter because of the great influence they have on our lives. Our people are either pointing us to Jesus or they are not. Can I rephrase that very important, underline-worthy truth into a question?

Are your friends pointing you to Jesus? How?

Are your friends influencing you in a positive way? Explain.

Do your friends make you better and point you to Jesus, or do they lead you to places of darkness and temptation?

The answer for some of you is painful. Maybe your friend group is mean and talks about others. Perhaps your group of friends is making poor decisions with alcohol and drugs. It may be that you are surrounded by friends who are making poor decisions with their boyfriends. These groups exist. Everywhere. Perhaps you are in one of them. Spoiler: Those friends are not pointing you to Jesus.

We were created for biblical community. We were created to live life together with like-minded people. To walk through the very best and worst days together. And God calls us to glorify Him through all we say and all we do—and that includes the friends we choose.

Today in Scripture we will see just how important biblical community was for Daniel. He was surrounded by some really incredible, Christlike, together-even-in-the-dark-times people. So let's get into chapter 2 of Daniel. This is a long one, but aloud in your group, read all of Daniel 2.

Things were never dull in Babylon. We are going to dig deep into the passage in our personal study this week, but I want us to hit on three main points today as we look at this chapter of Scripture as a group.

1. DANIEL SURROUNDED HIMSELF WITH LIKE-MINDED FRIENDS.

Daniel and his friends had already been through so much. And it doesn't stop here. Because of their shared faith in Christ, Daniel and his friends had a bond and a support system unlike any other. Because they shared faith in Christ and desired to honor Him with their lives, they saw the world through the same point of view. They bonded over shared experiences and a shared faith.

In the same way, it is so important for us to surround ourselves with friends who are going to look at the world with a biblical worldview just as we are called to. God uses His people to speak truth and love to one another. I cannot tell you how many times the Lord has used my very best friend to point me to Scripture and to the things of Jesus. It is an incredible gift.

2. DANIEL'S COMMUNITY SUPPORTED HIM.

Life is hard, isn't it? We face many different types of difficult seasons and trials day by day. What a joy it is to be able to face these trials and difficult days knowing we have our people by our side. In verse 17, Daniel went straight to his people in a time of difficulty and trouble.

Read Daniel 2:17 aloud.

What was the first thing they did together?

3. KING NEB'S COMMUNITY LET HIM DOWN.

King Nebuchadnezzar surrounded himself with a whole bunch of people, didn't he?

Who were the people King Neb went to for wisdom? List them here.

Isn't it interesting that out of all of these men and all of their "powers," none of them could deliver what the king sought? This is such a good picture for us. The key is not just to surround ourselves with people. Not just anybody. The key is to surround ourselves with a community of believers who love us like Jesus and support us as we seek to honor God with our lives.

Oh girls, friendships are hard. I hope you hear my heart when I say that one true, believing friend is of more value than one hundred fake ones. I want you to take some time to think about who your people are, and ask the Lord to help you identify the areas of your community where you might need to begin making some changes.

A NOTE TO THE GIRL WHO FEELS
TRAPPED IN A GROUP OF FRIENDS:

I understand you might feel like you are in the midst of a group of friends you cannot leave. It has taken you years to establish your space in this group, and you are not able to make changes that might shake up your status. You know you're all mean, but you aren't as mean as some. And perhaps this group has helped ensure that you have a handsome date for every school dance and function. Maybe this particular group of friends has helped you and watched you make some really bad choices, and you don't want to leave for fear of what they will say. I hear you. I see you. Those emotions are valid. But, sister, to stay where you are due to fear or shame is just letting the enemy keep you in the shackles that bind you! In Christ, we are free. Really free. From the chains that bind us to any group of people, reputation, or social status. I encourage you to trust God today and act as He leads. Don't let anyone, including yourself, hold you back from obedience. I am praying for you today.

A NOTE TO THE GIRL WHO FEELS
LIKE SHE HAS NO *PEOPLE*:

I see you. The one who is sitting there trying to hide the sting on your face when you feel that every other friend is pointing to everyone but you when they talk about who their people are. I understand that you feel like you are on an island, and you are nobody's number one girl. And I feel that it hurts you and causes you to question how you are supposed to have a biblical community when you seem to struggle to find community at all. The enemy may use this to make you feel poorly about yourself. To question why you are the way you are and to even make you want to change so that people might like you or want you around. Those are all lies. You are worthy of love and community just as you are. I am asking today for the Lord to specifically place someone in your path who might be a real friend. Praying for Him to provide you with peace while you wait and joy when He answers our prayers.

Before you leave your groups today, answer these questions and think about your answers:

Why does community matter? Explain.

Who are your people?

How do your people influence you?

Do your people point you to Jesus?

HERE & NOW

In the fall of 2016, my dad went into an emergency surgery at UAB hospital in Birmingham and came out six hours later on a ventilator entering into what would become a fight for his life. My mom, aunt, and I sat in a small hospital conference room with a surgeon we had never met, listening to her explain that our guy was in critical condition and that we would have to take it an hour at a time for the time being. My world was shaken. My heart was unsure of what would come next. All I knew was that I needed to call my people and ask them to pray.

Within minutes the waiting room was full of *our people*. Holding us. Praying over us. Feeding us. Speaking truth to us. They dove right into the pit with us and pulled us up for air.

I have never in my life experienced tangible biblical community like I did the year when we continued to stand alongside my dad in his battle against cancer. That is what our people do. They show up, stand with us, and point us to truth.

Isn't it incredible to try and picture Babylon? It sometimes sounds like a different world. Something we see in movies or read about in books filled with beautiful language and exotic descriptions of places.

What we read on the pages of Scripture is not fantasy. It is 100 percent truth. I want you to remember that as we dive into this chapter of study and learn more about the culture of Babylon and the way people lived and believed in the midst of it. Put those images of Diagon Alley and Cinderella's castle out of your mind, and let's dig into something real.

SECTION 1: TRUTH AND UNDERSTANDING
Daniel 2:1-16

In chapter two of the Book of Daniel, we meet King Neb in the second year of his reign. Scripture tells us he had dreams that troubled him. Before we move any further, take a moment to think about dreams you have had. I am not talking about the "I dream of one day winning the gold medal in pie eating..." or of "being the woman Tim Tebow decides he is made for." I mean the dreams you have when you fall asleep.

Are there any specific dreams you can recall? Any recurring dreams? Have you ever had a dream that evoked a great deal of emotion? Hurt you? Scared you? Troubled you? What emotions did you feel when you woke?

In my own sleep, I have often dreamed of big waves crashing down on me. Tidal waves. I have had several instances when I have woken up in an absolute panic after a giant wave crashed down on me in the middle of the ocean. Yikes!

So now that we have all relived our sweet dreams (and some bad dreams—tidal waves and all) together, it puts us in a better place to consider King Neb.

He had a bad dream. A troubling dream. And in true King Neb fashion, he wouldn't rest until he got what he wanted. In this case, he desired understanding. He wanted someone to explain to him exactly what his dream meant.

Read Daniel 2:1-16.

Who did the king call in to explain his dreams?

Were these men able to fulfill the king's order and explain the dream? Why or why not?

What was his reaction to this?

Take a moment to list the highlights of this passage.

Incredible! Girls. The king called in magicians, enchanters, and astrologers, and not one of them could make sense of the dreams the king had experienced.

Where do you look for wisdom? To whom do you go to for understanding?

Are you relying on cute quotes on Instagram for inspiration? Are you seeking answers in Facebook polls and GroupMe chats? Are you trusting your friends to interpret what the Lord is stirring in your soul?

King Neb was a man who was surrounded by voices, and none of what he was hearing was the truth.

Are you looking for wisdom and understanding in all of the wrong places? If not now, how have you done so in the past? What temptations to do this might you face in the future?

I encourage you to put a halt to that empty search. No longer look to the empty and false things for your truth. Instead, like Daniel, seek Jesus. He will be found. And He will provide for you all the truth and understanding you seek in His perfect timing.

You may be thinking—*Amy, I am not seeking out wisdom in magicians or sorcerers, but I also don't know where to find real truth.* I would encourage you to first start with Scripture. God's Word is fully alive and completely true. It is infallible and applicable for your life today. Seek God out in His Word! Then, pray! Ask God to reveal Himself to you through His Word. Our prayers do not have to be eloquent or well thought out. Talk with God and speak to Him the things in your heart and trust that He will reveal himself to you as you seek Him in this way. And, finally, seek truth from people who live out the truth!

I have spent many Saturday mornings with women who love Jesus and pour His truth into my life. Seek out people you know love God and honor Him with their lives. Let's fade out those empty voices and seek wisdom and understanding where it may truly be found!

SECTION 2: COMMUNITY CONTRAST
Daniel 2:12-19

Imagine with me for a moment where Daniel found himself. King Neb had dreams that troubled him. He called in all of the wise men he knew to explain the dreams to him. These men were unable to provide the answers King Neb desired. Since these men could not fulfill their purpose, the king declared that all the wise men of the kingdom must be killed.

Let's walk through this step by step.

> **12** Because of this, the king became violently angry and gave orders to destroy all the wise men of Babylon. **13** The decree was issued that the wise men were to be executed, and they searched for Daniel and his friends, to execute them. **14** Then Daniel responded with tact and discretion to Arioch, the captain of the king's guard, who had gone out to execute the wise men of Babylon. **15** He asked Arioch, the king's officer, "Why is the decree from the king so harsh?" Then Arioch explained the situation to Daniel. **16** So Daniel went and asked the king to give him some time, so that he could give the king the interpretation. **17** Then Daniel went to his house and told his friends Hananiah, Mishael, and Azariah about the matter, **18** urging them to ask the God of the heavens for mercy concerning this mystery, so Daniel and his friends would not be destroyed with the rest of Babylon's wise men. **19** The mystery was then revealed to Daniel in a vision at night, and Daniel praised the God of the heavens. **Daniel 2:12-19**

Underline the king's command after understanding wasn't provided by his wise men.

What unfolded in verses 16-19?

Again, Daniel responded to a command from King Nebuchadnezzar and stepped out in faith to honor God with his actions. Truth in action. Tangible obedience. Are you catching onto this theme yet?

All of a sudden Daniel found himself in a very tricky situation. As wise men, Daniel and his friends were to be killed alongside this group of men who had failed the king. Instead, Daniel asked for a meeting with the king and communicated that he could interpret the dream. What incredible faith! And he was not walking this road alone.

Underline verses 17 and 18.

Where did Daniel go for support in a time of huge need?

Picture it. People's lives were at stake. Daniel stepped out in obedience against the king, and then came back to his house for support and to pray with his friends, his brothers in Christ. What an incredible picture of community! We were created to live life together. The wonderful days and the difficult days. We were created to live life with people who will point us to Jesus. And these men did just that. They gathered and they prayed. Trusting God together.

Compare and contrast the men Daniel and King Nebuchadnezzar surrounded themselves with.

King Neb:

Daniel:

It is very clear that Daniel chose his community wisely. They spoke truth. They pointed him to trust God. On the other hand, King Neb surrounded himself with people who spoke empty truth over him and just said the things he wanted to hear.

Does any of that ring true in your life? How so?

Take a moment to think about the three people who are closest to you. Just like Daniel had his three friends he trusted most and went to in times of trial, who are the people you trust and seek during difficult times?

List their names and describe those friendships here.

What do you value most about your friendship with them?

How do they encourage you? How do they respond when you are in the midst of a trial?

As you read the following quote from *Bittersweet* by Shauna Niequist, I want to encourage you to reach out to your people and thank them. For walking through good days and bad days with you. For loving you. And, most of all, for pointing you to Jesus.

> "Everybody has a home team: it's the people you call when you get a flat tire or when something terrible happens. It's the people who, near or far, know everything that's wrong with you and love you anyway....These are the ones who tell you their secrets, who get themselves a glass of water without asking when they're at your house. These are the people who cry when you cry. These are your people, your middle-of-the-night, no-matter-what people."[1]

SECTION 3: PRAISE GOD
Daniel 2:20-24

I have the opportunity to work with girls like you on a regular basis. And when I say "work with" I mean I get to live life with them. We eat a lot of cheese dip, do a lot of crying, and seek Jesus together every day. Day in and day out.

I once walked one of my girls through a situation where she had to decide between two groups. She was so torn. Her heart could not land on one group without feeling as though she was abandoning another. Fears of judgment and disappointment made her decision a scary one. We sat in my office one afternoon and together we prayed that God would make her next step very clear. And guess what? He did. And she panicked.

My husband and I were walking into a movie one day, and I got a phone call from my teary girl toiling over her decision. I remember so clearly asking her, "Do you feel God has given you a clear answer?"

She said, "Yes!" And I responded simply, "Then praise Him for answering our prayers and trust Him as we walk forward in obedience."

I can only imagine Daniel feeling the same way. He gathered with his friends in their home and asked God to give wisdom and understanding in interpreting the dream for King Neb. In verse 19, we saw his prayer answered. And what Daniel did next was beautiful.

> **20** Blessed be the name of God forever and ever, to whom belong wisdom and might. **21** He changes times and seasons; he removes kings and sets up kings; he gives wisdom to the wise and knowledge to those who have understanding; **22** he reveals deep and hidden things; he knows what is in the darkness, and the light dwells with him. **23** To you, O God of my fathers, I give thanks and praise, for you have given me wisdom and might, and have now made known to me what we asked of you, for you have made known to us the king's matter. **Daniel 2:20-23**

Daniel praised God. His God who gives all wisdom and understanding. His God whose timing is perfect. This praise to God sums up the theme of the entire Book of Daniel. And the God who provided for Daniel at just the right time is the God who will do the same for you.

FAST FACT: This is not the only time God revealed secrets in dreams. He did this for Joseph in Egypt. Read Genesis 40:8–41:16 to learn more.

How do you respond when God answers your prayers? Do you even notice when it happens?

Do you acknowledge and say thank you when God provides all that you need?

May we be followers of Christ who are known for praising our King! We seek understanding. We seek knowledge. We seek answers. We seek Him. And we find Him.

Our response each time we find Him should be to praise Him. He is the only One who is worthy of our praise. Let's end today praising God. Consider journaling a prayer of thanks and praise. Or you can speak it or sing it! Whatever you do—take some time now to say thank you to our God who is so worthy.

_____

_____

_____

_____

_____

SECTION 4: RESPOND
Daniel 2:24-30

God made known to Daniel the meaning of the dream, and Daniel took this wisdom straight to King Nebuchadnezzar.

Read Daniel 2:24-30.

Write out verses 27 and 28 below.

Circle the phrase "but there is a God in heaven," and underline it. Now underline it again.

Arioch was eager to claim the credit for bringing Daniel to the king to interpret the dream. Daniel was very clear in letting the king know that God was the one who revealed the mystery. Daniel had no wisdom on his own, but God provided him with all of the wisdom he needed.

List all the places King Neb sought wisdom.

Where was true wisdom found?

God gave insight to Daniel to interpret the dream so the king would know there was a true God who controlled all things.

Sister, I don't know what mysteries you are in the middle of. I don't know what understanding and wisdom you seek. Some of you may be trying to understand why someone very close to you has passed away or is very sick. Others may be walking through the depths of depression and seek understanding about why you have to walk this path, or wonder when you will see light at the end of the tunnel.

Some of you are walking around with broken hearts, and others might be battling an addiction that has you bound up so tightly you cannot breathe. Maybe you didn't get into the college of your dreams, or maybe your best friend is dating your ex-boyfriend and all of the plans you made suddenly feel out of reach.

Mysteries. All of them. The hurt and the hate and the confusion.

Dear one, there is a God in heaven who reveals mysteries. In His time. In His way. For your good. For His glory. And none of that is a mystery to Him.

I love these words written by Paul in Colossians.

> **1** For I want you to know how greatly I am struggling for you, for those in Laodicea, and for all who have not seen me in person. **2** I want their hearts to be encouraged and joined together in love, so that they may have all the riches of complete understanding and have the knowledge of God's mystery—Christ. **3** In him are hidden all the treasures of wisdom and knowledge. **Colossians 2:1-3**

Just like King Nebuchadnezzar, all of the answers you seek are hidden in the things of Christ.

Circle the word *treasures* in the passage above.

A treasure is something of great value or worth. And I would say that knowledge and understanding are of great value and worth to us. This week, I have challenged you to identify all of the empty voices and false truths in your life. Today, I am going to ask you to surrender them, and in their place, surround yourself with voices of truth.

I want you to take some time as we close out this week to journal.

What "mysteries" plague you?

What are the unanswered questions you have that cause you to struggle to trust Christ?

What is it you are waiting to know before you place your trust fully in Jesus?

Our God is a God of understanding and knowledge. And that is only found when we seek Him with all of our hearts. We will dive into what giving our hearts fully to Jesus looks like next week. For now, write your heart out.

unshaking faith

Faith in _____. What it looks like to put what we believe into practice in real-life situations.

Who is this _____ that can rescue you from my power? **Daniel 3:15c**

What idols are you being asked to bow to?

We're not facing a furnace, but we're definitely _____ _____ to _____.

Why were they not afraid of the furnace?

Our face _____ the faith of others.

Use the space provided to note any Scripture references or comments from the video you want to remember.

let's talk

There are parts of your life you do not want me to know about. Stories you hope your friends and family never hear of. Things you have said that you never want repeated. So do I.

We all have things we tuck way in the back of our hearts. Hidden and kept secret for fear that the people around us will leave us or judge us if they find out. If they really knew, they might not want you anymore. If they saw what was in the depths of your heart, they might run. I worry about these things too.

This week is tough. It is personal. Scripture illuminates the dark places we hope no one will ever see. God is faithful and merciful in that way. He brings light to the darkest places. Hope to the pieces of our hearts near death.

I want you to pull up your boots and be willing to trek into some deep places with me. Are you excited? You should be. I am a very, very trustworthy guide. (This is not necessarily true in all areas of life. Do not ever take directions from me. Just don't. Google maps. Every time.)

We have spent the last two weeks digging into the Book of Daniel, identifying the culture we live in and the people we share that culture with. God has placed us in the midst of our culture for specific reasons. The people we surround ourselves with matter. This week, through the lens of Scripture, we will be called to take a look at our hearts and what might be stopping us from loving God with an undivided heart.

Talk through these questions together:

1. What is the first thing you think about in the morning?

2. What or who in life are you most afraid to lose?

3. Am I willing to lose my life for the sake of Christ?

I am not afraid to tell you my answers.

1. First thing I think about in the morning?
   Two-part answer: A) Do I have to wash my hair today? B) Is there a cold Diet Coke in the fridge?

2. What or who am I most afraid to lose?

My husband and my son.

3. Am I willing to lose my life for the sake of Christ?

Sisters, my answer is *yes*. It is an absolute *yes*. But I toiled over this. I had never in my years considered this as I should have. I had never sat myself down and considered my life and the details of it, and then asked myself if I would surrender that for the sake of Jesus. Tears and tears. Yes, Lord. For You. Yes. But, wow.

Here is where I found myself next. If I am willing to literally lay down my life for Christ, then why am I not willing to lay down my phone to spend uninterrupted time in His Word? Why am I not willing to give up an hour of sleep for the sake of seeking Him in prayer? Why am I unwilling to forget my schedule and go out of my way to love my neighbor? Lose things like friends, affection, reputation, and invitations in order to honor God with my life?

This is the perfect time to meet three men in the fiery furnace. Actually, let's study for a moment how they got there. In your groups, read all 30 verses of Daniel chapter 3 and walk through the following questions:

What did King Nebuchadnezzar build?

What did the king ask everyone in Babylon to do?

How did Shadrach, Meshach, and Abednego respond?

What would you have done?

Have you ever found yourself in a situation like this? Explain.

Picture this for a moment. King Neb had an image of gold built that reflected the enormous statue from his dream. It was 90 feet high and 9 feet wide; this is half as tall as Cinderella's castle or five times the height of a giraffe. This image of gold was huge and was meant to assert that there would be no other kingdoms after his.

I sure can't. I remember not wanting to ever be the only one standing in the lunchroom while everyone else was eating, let alone being the only one out of thousands not bowing to an idol.

So, what was the deal? Was not bowing to this idol really worth risking the lives of these men? Yes. It was. Why? Because by bowing they would have been communicating to everyone around them that they believed there was a power outside of the power of God. They were unwilling to bow to anyone but their mighty God.

Now is the time you all are thinking, *"That's a super interesting story, Ames, but nobody is ever going to ask my entire city to bow down to a tall metal structure five times the size of a giraffe."* Sister, that may be true. But I can guarantee you, at some point or another, you will be asked to bow. To pressure. To people. Each of us has things that we will bow our hearts to.

The word *bow* means to bend in reverence and submission.[1] To what or to whom are you bending in submission? Each of us has allowed idols to grow in our hearts. We have built a tower to something other than Jesus. Our hearts have allowed territory to be taken by things that should not be. You have idols. I have idols. And we are bowing down to them every day.

FAITH OVER FEAR

In the first part of chapter 3, King Neb made it clear what the people were supposed to do when they heard the sound of the music. They were all supposed to bow. Shadrach, Meshach, and Abednego refused to bow, and did not hesitate in their decision. A group of people made this known to the king, and he decided to call them in and confront them about their rebellion.

Read aloud Daniel 3:13-18.

In your own words, record what these three men said to the king when he threatened their lives if they did not bow.

Incredible! These men were being threatened with their lives and they did not give up. They did not give in. How simple would it have been for them to let fear take over and just bow down to appease the king? But, no. They chose to look fear in the face and lay down their lives for the sake of honoring God.

We will dig more into that and how we can apply their boldness to our lives in the personal study days coming up this week. There is so much we can take away from this moment in the king's court.

UNWAVERING TRUST

King Nebuchadnezzar made a big turnaround in this passage. He was first filled with rage that the three men would not bow to his golden image and went so far as to challenge "their God" to save them. As we have seen, these men did get thrown into the fiery furnace. A furnace that was heated seven times more than usual due to the king's fury. The fire was so hot and brutal that the men who carried them to the doors were killed. All reason and logic would say these men would die. That this was the end of their lives. But there is a God in heaven, and He met them right there in the fiery furnace.

In Daniel 3:24-25, we see a fourth individual in the furnace. We will study this more in our personal study, but for right now I want you to see that God showed up. Right there in the midst of their trial. They were untouched. Unharmed. Girls, they didn't even smell of smoke. God is with us in trial. What a testimony of the power of God!

And oh, how quickly King Neb went from mocking the God of Shadrach, Meshach, and Abednego to praising Him. In verse 28, the king spoke blessings to God, but his heart was not truly changed. What a fickle heart. One that praises God in some moments and speaks ill of Him the next.

My hope is for you to see the unwavering trust Shadrach, Meshash, and Abednego had in God no matter their circumstances. They loved God and trusted Him with all of their hearts.

Spend some time at the end of group today working through these questions.

What are the areas of your life where idols have been built?

Are you willing to address these idols? Why or why not?

Where do you put your faith?

Why is trusting God scary?

When has God sustained you in the midst of trials?

How did that sharpen your faith?

HERE & NOW

If you have spent any time with me, you know Corrie ten Boom is one of my heroes. Her story changed my life. She was born an ordinary woman in a normal family and ended up facing a life filled with trials she never could have anticipated.

Corrie and her family helped many Jews escape the Nazi Holocaust during World War II. I wish that I could sit down with you and tell you the stories I have read about her life and her trust in Jesus. She had an unwavering faith in an extraordinary God. My eyes fill with tears thinking of the horrors she and so many others endured during that time.

In my favorite book of all time, *The Hiding Place*, we read details of the life and faith of Corrie and her family during this time. One of my favorite quotes from the book is this:

> "My job was simply to follow His leading one step at a time, holding every decision up to Him in prayer." [2]

Incredible faith. She knew that her role was to be obedient to God and have faith in Him. She trusted Him every step of the way.

Do you see your life through this lens? Does it scare you to be called to a life of faith, trusting God with every step?

Describe a specific time when you've had to live with extraordinary faith through a really difficult time.

personal study

SECTION 1: EYES OUT FOR IDOLS
Daniel 3:1-5

Idols weren't hard to spot in Babylon. In fact, they were designed and built in such a way that they could not be missed. Chapter 3 begins with King Nebuchadnezzar and an image of gold that he meant for all the peoples and nations to bow down to and worship. We discussed in our group session that this idol was made of pure gold, standing 90-feet-tall and was positioned in a place where it could not be missed.

> **FAST FACT:** The chapter repeatedly states this was the image the king set up. It is unclear whether the image was of King Neb or of one of the gods that he worshiped.

King Neb was making a statement here. His kingdom. His reign. He was not going anywhere and was not planning on sharing power at any time.

Read Daniel 3:1-5.

Who did King Neb gather together to attend the dedication of the golden image?

It is interesting to me that the king gathered such a noble and important group of individuals to attend the dedication of this idol. And even more interesting that, when the music sounded, they all bowed.

Can you think of moments in our world and our culture when important individuals (celebrities, politicians, officials) bow? Explain.

Have you ever done something or taken on an opinion as your own just because someone important said so? Why?

In our everyday life, the idols aren't always going to be as obvious as a giant image of gold set up in our city. (In some cases, however, they may be.) We most likely won't have a 90-foot structure placed in our yard to bow down to. For us, the idols may be harder to spot. More challenging for us to pick out of our everyday lives.

But they are there. Gaining root in our heart. Placing distance between our hearts and the things of Jesus. And they are dangerous.

Think about how much Shadrach, Meshach, and Abednego were willing to risk by refusing to bow down to idols. Their lives. They were literally thrown into a furnace. Their lives to be put to an end.

But us. Me? Often, I treat my idols with kid gloves.

Do I put things before the Lord? Do I let idols grow in my heart and mind? Sure, but I try not to let it take over too much. I think about it sometimes. I consider giving it up. I write in my prayer journal about addressing it. But girls, this is not battling idols. This is hosting them. This is setting up houses for them. This is knowing they are near and making room for them in our lives.

I am asking you—imploring you—begging you. Stop hosting idols in your heart. Let's be young women who fight idols rather than befriend them.

You may be saying, "Amy, I don't even know where to begin in identifying idols."

An idol is any object of worship besides God. As believers of Jesus Christ, all of our worship and affection is to be given to God. Anything else that receives our worship or affection is an idol in our lives. Use the following statements to help you identify areas where idols may be hiding. Place a mark on the scale that best indicates how closely the statement describes you.

If I fail an examine or don't get an A on a paper, I am frustrated and upset.

Strongly Agree · Strongly Disagree

If my life doesn't look picture perfect, I can't post it on my social media.

Strongly Agree · Strongly Disagree

If I don't succeed in sports or am not recognized for my achievements, I am frustrated and upset.

Strongly Agree · Strongly Disagree

If I don't have the ideal body image, I am frustrated and upset.

Strongly Agree · Strongly Disagree

I encourage you to take a few minutes to consider these things in your heart. Study your answers, and consider what you may be allowing to stand as an idol in your life.

What idols are you bowing to?

Are you afraid to deal with them? Why or why not?

Take some time to journal about the emptiness of idols and reflect on Daniel 3:1-5. Ask God to open your eyes to idols in your heart and life that you need to surrender to Him. Then pause and take a break (maybe go for a walk or a bike ride), and then join me back here for the next section of personal study.

SECTION 2: ADDRESSING IDOLS
Daniel 3:16-18

Remember at the beginning of the group session when I warned you that I want us to allow the Lord to drag all of the things we have been hiding out into the light? Today is the day when we take inventory and start to fight. Idols cannot be ignored. They cannot be put away for later. Idols are dangerous. Life-threatening.

Y'all. I hate what I am about to do to you because I know where your brain will go. But the analogy works, so sorry for the nightmares.

Let's say that I knock on your door and drop off a giant spider. I am talking *huge*. Like cat size. No box. No cage. Just a free-roaming spider to do what he pleases in your house. Sure, this is the place where you come to rest and sleep and eat and be spider-free. But not anymore. Hello spider.

Would you be able to rest? To sit and be at ease? To feel at peace?

Next scenario. And again, I'm sorry. But what if you were sitting in your living room in your house at night by yourself, and you heard a door open and shut.

Panic. You would panic. Why? Because you sense danger. Something is not right. Something is in your house that should not be there, and you do not feel safe.

Do you feel a little anxious right now? Anybody putting their feet up to get away from spiders and locking their doors to make sure nobody can get in?

Sister, we should feel the same way about our idols. Our hearts should feel uneasy. We should not be okay with the sin we are allowing to take up residence in our safe places. And it is sin that we are allowing to creep in and create a barrier in our hearts between us and the things of Jesus. These idols exist and it's time to extinguish them by facing them head on.

Shadrach, Meshach, and Abednego were forced to face an idol head on. Literally. Let's take a look at their bold words as they stood up to the king.

> **16** Shadrach, Meshach, and Abednego replied to the king, "Nebuchadnezzar, we don't need to give you an answer to this question. **17** If the God we serve exists, then he can rescue us from the furnace of blazing fire, and he can rescue us from the power of you, the king. **18** But even if he does not rescue us, we want you as king to know that we will not serve your gods or worship the gold statue you set up."
> **Daniel 3:16-18**

Underline the phrase: "he can rescue us from the power of you."

And then circle the phrase: "we will not serve your gods or worship the gold statue you set up."

These men knew what was at stake. Their lives. And even then, they were looking their idols in the face and fighting them—trusting that their God would protect them.

Was it easy? No. Was it without risk? No. Was it simple? No.

But it was obedient and brought glory to God. And God honored their faithfulness. We must put our faith in God and battle our idols too.

You may need to break up with a boyfriend. Battling your idols might mean you need to say *no* the next time you are offered that drug or that drink. Or it might mean you need to tell someone that you need help with an addiction. It could also mean it's time for you to give up on having the perfect score on that standardized test. Or put away the dreams of being a size 2 with perfect hair. Delete your Snapchat. Whatever it is that has built up a tower in your heart, it is time to knock it down. It is time to look it straight in the face and remove it.

And you do not have to do it on your own. Just as He was for the three men in the furnace, God will be with you every step.

SECTION 3: OUR GOD DELIVERS
Daniel 3:23-30

In the fall of 2016, I found myself in the waiting room of an intensive care unit with a surgeon telling members of my family that my dad was very ill. He was on a ventilator in the Surgical ICU of our local hospital and our instructions were to take it hour by hour to see how my dad progressed.

This was a moment in my life when I can honestly say I felt that all of the world was crashing down on me. My heart beat faster. My breathing was shallow. My brain didn't know what to think. It was the greatest amount of fear that I had ever felt in all of my life.

I remember walking out onto a patio of the hospital to have a moment away from all of the people. I took a deep breath and said out loud "Deliver us, God. Save us from where we are."

In the midst of fear, all my heart knew to do was cry out to the one who could abolish every hurt and heal any ailment. The God I cried out to in faith to deliver me in my moment of fear is the same God who Shadrach, Meshach, and Abednego trusted to deliver them from the fiery furnace all those years ago.

> On a scale of one to ten, how scared would you have been to be thrown into a fiery furnace?

Umm ... is 200 an option? I would be terrified! But these men trusted that their God would deliver them. Without hesitation. And deliver them He did!

Read Daniel 3:23-30.

Then pray, asking God to give you wisdom and to help you better understand His Word this week. Let's work through the Scripture together.

> **23** And these three men, Shadrach, Meshach, and Abednego fell, bound, into the furnace of blazing fire. **24** Then King Nebuchadnezzar jumped up in alarm. He said to his advisers, "Didn't we throw three men, bound, into the fire?" "Yes, of course, Your Majesty," they replied to the king. **25** He exclaimed, "Look! I see four men, not tied, walking around in the fire unharmed; and the fourth looks like a son of the gods."
> **Daniel 3:23-25**

Girls, not only did God deliver them from the furnace and spare their lives, but God was present *in the fire* with them. God has promised us that He will be with us. And that He would deliver us. How sweet it is to see that promise kept so clearly in this passage of Scripture.

Have you ever walked through a day when you have had to cling to faith that God would deliver?

How did God strengthen your trust and faith in Him through this trial?

Reflect on God's presence and how we should trust Him with our worries and fears. List any worries and fears you need to lay down at His feet. Remember He cares for you and knows exactly what you are going through.

Read 1 Peter 5:6-9.

Worry and fear are sin. We must cast our cares on Him and be alert, as verse 8 says, because the enemy seeks to devour.

How are we to respond and act (v. 9)?

Are these sufferings unique to you? Who else is facing trials according to verse 9?

Deliverance doesn't always come right away or exactly when we expect it. Sometimes we must be patient and wait for God's deliverance.

Thanks for sticking with the personal study for this session. Go for a walk, and then come back and continue in your personal study.

SECTION 4: BUT IF NOT…

I know what some of you are thinking.

I have had faith, but…
- my mom is still sick.
- my friends still left me.
- my boyfriend broke my heart.
- I still haven't made anything I've tried out for.
- the acceptance letter still hasn't come.
- my parents are still getting divorced.

You may be struggling to have faith because you feel that God has not kept His end of the deal. Or you may worry that He has forgotten about you. Or perhaps you struggle with believing that He truly cares.

Sister, I have been there. Most of us can testify that we have struggled with the same worries and fears of being forgotten and abandoned. Those whispers you hear in your head and your heart telling you that God isn't worth seeking or trusting are lies from the enemy—an enemy who wants you to give up on your faith in God and instead take things into your own hands.

I want to remind you today that you, yes *you*, have a mighty God who fights for *you*. He loves *you* so much that He sent His only Son to die for *you*. He cares about the details of your days, and He goes before you and maps out your path. And His path for you is good. Yes, it's difficult, and sometimes it's very scary. But His path for you is good.

I can only imagine the fear Shadrach, Meshach, and Abednego felt as they faced the furnace.

Take a moment to write out Daniel 3:16-18 (ESV).

Now, circle the words "but if not…"

Have you ever had a moment like these men? Journal about it here if
you have.

_____

_____

_____

_____

_____

Have you ever found yourself in the midst of a trial and had to look fear in the face and say,
"I may not get the healing I was hoping for; I may not get the answer I was hoping for; I may
not get the relationship I was hoping for; I may not get the family I was hoping for ..."?

But if not, I still will not bow. I will not give in. I will not lose faith.

What circumstances do you find yourself in right now that you need to
surrender to the Lord?

In what areas are you struggling to have faith?

_____

_____

_____

_____

_____

_____

_____

_____

_____

_____

Take some time at the end of this week and work through the squares below. Be honest here. This is a time for you to process out loud—express and acknowledge through writing—the areas where you need to have bold faith, even in fear. I've given you a few ideas to get you started.

I may not get the relationship I was hoping for	But if not
I may not get the answer I was looking for	But if not
I may not get into the college of my dreams	But if not
I may not	But if not
I may not	But if not
I may not	But if not
I may not	But if not
I may not	But if not

influencers

press play

What did King Nebuchadnezzar want in the first chapters of Daniel?

Whose faith influenced King Neb?

What is Daniel known for?

Through his dream, God is calling King Nebuchadnezzar to _____ himself.

How many months pass between the king's dream and the consequences of his pride and lack of humility?

God is the only _____ that reigns.

Use the space provided to note any Scripture references or comments from the video you want to remember.

let's talk

Have I mentioned to you that I have my dream job? I mean the dream of Amy Houston Byrd's life? Every day I have the opportunity to serve as the Director of Girls' Ministry at my home church in Birmingham. It makes me smile just typing it. I cannot believe the Lord has seen fit for me to live life with and love these precious girls in my care.

We go on church mission trips and retreats and ride roller coasters and do crafts...all together! We get coffee. We eat lots of cheese dip. They spend a lot of time in my office. It is a lot of togetherness. And we love it. (Fun fact: I am typing this from a charter bus right this moment and the girls sitting behind me are mocking me because I don't know the words to a One Direction song. Sorry.)

In our abundance of time together I have noticed a trend. Sometimes they act like me. They mimic what they see me do. They measure their life to how my life (a season or ten ahead of them) is going.

One of the funniest things is when the girls do or say or even wear things that make them, as they say, "look like Amy." I wish you could see it like I do. For example, I call everyone pumpkin head. I mean *everyone*. If I met the Queen of England, I just might say, "It is so nice to meet you, Your Majesty, cute little pumpkin head!" Recently, I was spending time with a group of my high school girls, and I heard several of them say it. "Hey pumpkin head!" And it hit me: They hear me. They know me.

Whether they know it or not—even in silly ways—I influence them. In more serious ways, they have heard me quote a specific passage of Scripture over them. They've also heard stories from my life that they will apply to their own. They know my heart has been broken in relationships. And in turn, some of them apply the lessons I have learned to their own world.

They love my husband and my baby boy, and in turn, will say that they cannot wait to have a "little family just like [mine]."

My life, every part of it, influences those girls. Influence means the power to change or affect someone or something. Look around you. All sorts of things influence us.

How might the following things influence you: Commercials on TV? Celebrities? Social media? Music? Politicians?

Our place influences us. It changes us. It affects us. It shapes who we are. Our people influence us.

We spent a lot of time studying this in session two. The people we spend most of our time with are inevitably going to influence us! This week, I want to take a look at the influence we have on the people around us.

You have influence. Sister, did you know that you can change the world? Yes, you. You were meant to be a world changer! The Lord created you to fulfill a purpose on this planet that no other person can accomplish.

Your life matters. Your voice is meant to be heard. You are special. You are valuable. God purposed you to influence people with your life in very intentional ways. He put you as you are, where you are, and with the people you are with for a reason.

Let that sink in. Stop looking at the other girls in your group and your school and your city and waiting for their impact. I am looking at *you*!

There are people in your life who you are influencing right now. It could be a younger sibling, a friend at school, or even a coach for a team you play on. It might be a person in your math class who knows you are a believer and is watching how you live. Maybe it is a friend who knows you love Jesus and is confused by the way you live.

Who are you influencing?

You are meant to influence others—to make an impact—to change other people for the better.

We may not always understand why we are where we are. Some of you may be very unhappy and frustrated about where you are. That is understandable. And you would not be the first person in a place, surrounded by a people, with a task you didn't expect or even enjoy.

Can you imagine how Daniel and his friends must have felt?

Taken from their home in Judah. Kidnapped. No choice at all. Placed in a new city. A role in King Neb's army placed on them. Surrounded by different and altogether unfamiliar people. The Lord literally moved them from what they knew and placed them in a turbulent kingdom with a cruel king for one purpose: to influence. And out of all the men in all the world, the Lord chose Daniel to give wisdom and understanding to the dreams this cruel king was having. It was a very specific assignment.

I want us to compare two men who were leaders in their own right.

Read Daniel chapter 4 together as a group.

List some characteristics of the leadership of King Neb and Daniel:

Nebuchadnezzar	Daniel

Daniel wasn't looking to be in a place of power. He was not seeking out authority and certainly did not desire to have direct audiences with the king. But God had plans for Daniel's influence to be greater and louder than he imagined.

Daniel's obedience to God and his humility in the way he lived were what influenced others most. King Neb was a different story entirely. He longed to be worshiped, noticed, adored, and in control. He boasted in himself and demanded others to bow to him.

Daniel 4:30 is a perfect example of this pride that ran deep in King Neb's heart.

> The king exclaimed, "Is this not Babylon the Great that I have built to
> be a royal residence by my vast power and for my majestic glory?"
> **Daniel 4:30**

Circle the portions of this verse that communicate the king's pride.

Girls, I don't know about you, but if I'm honest, I believe I act more like King Neb than I act like Daniel more often than I would like to admit. I want people to notice when I do good works. My heart longs for someone to tell me I am talented and for others to see how hard I am trying. I look around and wait for someone to compliment my fancy shoes and pretty hair and clean house.

None of those are bad things on their own. The longing in my heart to be known is not bad. It is natural. But the root of that is pride in my heart. It is sin when I make it about me. And the Lord addressed the pride of King Neb, didn't he?

What happened to King Neb when he continued to boast in himself?

Our only boast should be in Christ. Our only hope of really influencing others—of changing the world—is when Christ is the center of all that we do and the One we are doing it for.

King Neb influenced others. But he did not influence others in positive ways. He did not influence others in ways that made them better. On the other hand, Daniel influenced others humbly and all for the sake of honoring God.

You are meant to be a world changer. You are meant to change people because of how God has changed you.

As we close our time together, answer these questions as a group and share your answers with one another.

Who influences you?

Who are you influencing?

Are you influencing from a place of pride like King Neb or a place of humility like Daniel?

HERE & NOW

My grandfather changed my life. He was a simple man who loved God and his family stronger than anyone I have ever known. If you ever had the joy of meeting Glynn Houston, you knew the details of his family and were most likely invited to his home church.

Everyone he encountered was changed for the better.

As his granddaughter, I got a front row seat to his life. The way he loved his wife, my beloved grandmother. The way he loved his kids, my dad, and my aunt. And the way he loved his grandchildren and the rest of his very large extended family.

The way I love today is because of the way I saw him love. His life changed mine. And I hope I am able to influence my people to love God and others the same way my grandfather influenced me.

Who has influenced you?

In what ways did their influence impact your life?

How has their influence changed the way you love others?

personal study

SECTION 1: WISDOM FROM GOD
Daniel 4:1-28

Chapter four is interesting because it begins with a letter of praise to God. Let that sink in for a moment. The man who sentenced men to death in a fiery furnace was praising God and expressing awe in His signs and wonders!

Take a moment to write out Daniel 4:3.

It is so interesting to me that King Neb was writing of the everlasting kingdom of God. A man who built idols and whose kingdom was the center of his life was speaking of a different kingdom—the true kingdom of God. It seems that the Lord might have been up to something in the heart of this cruel king.

In verses 4-16, we read the details of a second dream King Nebuchadnezzar had.

Draw a picture of the dream he described in this passage.

What a dream!

Who did the king call on first to interpret the dream?

Who ultimately was able to interpret the dream?

The dream spoke of a mighty tree, and Daniel shared that this represented the king. In the dream, the cosmic tree would be cut to the ground and left as a stump. This represented the removal of the king's influence and glory.

And it didn't stop there. This dream showed the king would not only lose his power and glory, but he would also lose the rationality that distinguished him as human, leaving him to behave as an animal. This would bring him to a place of humility like none other—a reminder that he was merely human, and not god-like, after all.

> What does the passage say would be allowed to remain of the tree that had been cut down?
> _____ and _____.

This image suggests that Nebuchadnezzar's kingdom would be protected while he learned to show honor to the true God.

Wow. This news, even in dream form, must have been terrifying to a king who had built an entire kingdom to please and honor himself. Daniel, in obedience to what God had revealed to him, went on to give the following words of wisdom to King Nebuchadnezzar.

> Therefore, may my advice seem good to you my king. Separate yourself from your sins by doing what is right, and from your injustices by showing mercy to the needy. Perhaps there will be an extension of your prosperity. **Daniel 4:27**

Daniel was willing to tell this cruel king the truth no matter what his response would be.

Consider what you know about Nebuchadnezzar so far, and think about how he might have taken these words from Daniel, who had just told him: End your sin. Pursue righteousness. Show mercy.

These words the Lord gave to Daniel were bold, strong, and timely in the life of King Neb. Now, that is influence!

You may never have to look into the face of a king and tell him he must change his ways, but in order to influence others for the sake of Christ, you will have to face difficult situations and have tough conversations.

If we want to change the world—if we want to influence others—we must have a willing and obedient heart like Daniel. We must humbly ask God to equip us and then take on each assignment as it comes, trusting He will meet us there and give us all the wisdom and knowledge we need.

In our group time, I asked you to consider who you were influencing. Whose name did you write down? I want you to take it a step further now and journal *how* you are influencing this person.

Daniel could have just been there for the king and interpreted the dream without giving him the charge we see in verse 27. It would have been easier that way. But the Lord gave Daniel a specific word for a specific man at a specific time, and he walked in obedience to that call.

Has the Lord put you in a place at this time with a specific person to share boldly about Jesus?

Is it time for you to trust God to equip you as you dive into the life of someone to help her make a change?

The Lord will build up and sustain those who seek to change the world for the sake of bringing glory to Himself. And as we will see in our next section, the Lord will cut off those who seek to change the world for the purpose of making more of themselves.

SECTION 2: INFLUENCE & DOWNFALL
Daniel 4:28-33

Spoiler alert: Nebuchadnezzar's dream was not just a dream, it was a warning. A warning for the king to lay down his pride and his ways and turn to Jesus. An instruction spoken through Daniel by God telling the king what would happen if he did not surrender himself.

But the king ignored the words of warning and continued in sin. He continued on living in his palace, leading his people, and worshiping gods that were not real.

What we see next is this:

1. Our God will not be ignored.

2. Our God does not make false promises.

3. Our God does not let our sin go unaddressed.

4. Our God reigns and rules and will humble those who don't humble themselves.

One year after Daniel interpreted the dream and challenged the king to turn from his ways, Nebuchadnezzar remained the same.

I want to spend a lot of time today interacting with the following Scripture:

> **28** All this happened to King Nebuchadnezzar. **29** At the end of twelve months, as he was walking on the roof of the royal palace in Babylon, **30** the king exclaimed, "Is this not Babylon the Great that I have built to be a royal residence by my vast power and for my majestic glory?" **31** While the words were still in the king's mouth, a voice came from heaven: "King Nebuchadnezzar, to you it is declared that the kingdom has departed from you. **32** You will be driven away from people to live with the wild animals, and you will feed on grass like cattle for seven periods of time, until you acknowledge that the Most High is ruler over human kingdoms, and he gives them to anyone he wants." **33** At that moment the message against Nebuchadnezzar was fulfilled. He was driven away from people. He ate grass like cattle, and his body was drenched with dew from the sky, until his hair grew like eagles' feathers and his nails like birds' claws. **Daniel 4:28-33**

In verse 28, we see the king on the roof of his palace in Babylon. I want to help you visualize this with me. Remember how beautiful this city is. How extravagant. The view from the roof of his royal palace was probably something like you would see in a movie. He might have seen ornate temples, the famous "hanging gardens," which ancient Greeks considered one of the seven wonders of the world, and the enormous outer wall of his city.[1]

Keep in mind one year prior he had a terrifying dream and was warned by Daniel to turn from his ways and humble himself.

What did the king do in verse 30?

Circle where the Lord intervened.

This moment was powerful. Tangible. As the king is standing atop his palace boasting of his own works, the Lord spoke. And in an instant, the kingdom he saw was no longer his. The people no longer his people. The crown no longer his crown.

In your own words, describe where the Lord sent the king and in what state he was to live.

Reread verse 25 and see how it compares to what came true for the king.

Can you imagine how King Nebuchadnezzar must have felt? He went from having everything in his grasp to living among the animals.

What lesson do you think the Lord was teaching King Nebuchadnezzar?

So here we find the king. Without a kingdom. Without a crown. Humbled to the point of sharing a home with the beasts of the field.

Circle the words you think best describe how he must how felt at the time.

Desperate	Alone	Free	Happy
Scared	Comfortable	Hopeless	Low

Have you ever had a moment in your life like this? A moment when you found yourself at the end of your rope? In a place where you felt hopeless and desperate because of the consequences of your own sin?

Describe a time when you've experienced a moment like this.

We have studied and seen how the Lord gave Daniel position and authority because of his humility and obedience to God. And now we are sitting with a king in a pig sty.

Which person do you identify with?

Are you without true friends and real relationships because you let your social status become more important than loving others well? Are you not being selected at school tryouts because you put others down or treat them poorly for the sake of building yourself up? Has the cause of making yourself known become more important than making Christ known? Has Christ ever been your center, or have you been wearing a crown of pride all this time?

In God's grace, He did not make King Nebuchadnezzar stay in the pig sty. And you don't have to stay there either. The Lord clearly communicated with the king what it would take to get his kingdom back (v. 32).

Fill in the blanks for verse 32b.
Until you acknowledge that the _____ _____ is _____ _____ _____
_____ , and he gives them to _____ _____ _____ .

Surrender. Of pride. Of plans. Of self. This is what God called King Neb to do in order to gain his kingdom back.

Sister, I doubt you have a kingdom. But you do have a valuable life. Do not sit in a pig sty when you can live as a daughter of the true King. My prayer this day is for you to know the Most High rules in your life. He is the King of your heart. And any reign you have given yourself must be extinguished.

Go somewhere fun with a friend. Chat about life and share what you're learning from the Book of Daniel. Then come back and we'll continue in verses 34-37.

SECTION 3: EYES TO HEAVEN
Daniel 4:34-37

Our last section was heavy. I challenged you to surrender your life to God—the true King. Not only that, but I also challenged you to put truth into action every day.

That's what God does to us. He comes in and interrupts our routines in order to make us more like Him. I am not saying this is an easy task—to give up the reigns. In fact, I can guarantee it will be uncomfortable and painful at times. I can very clearly recall moments of my life when I've had to acknowledge that I let pride get in the way of my relationship with Jesus. I thought I knew better. I was sure my plans were best. The process was painful, but it was worth it.

Some of you might know exactly what I'm talking about. The Lord has cut you to a stump. You have been found at the end of yourself.

As King Nebuchadnezzar learned, that's right where we meet our God.

Read Daniel 4:34-37.

Circle the phrase "looked up to heaven" in your Bible.

Remember King Neb went from living in a palace to living among the animals. God humbled him. And after a season of testing and trying, this man who was once king humbly looked up to heaven and praised the one true King.

What happened when he raised his eyes to heaven (v. 34)?

Take a moment to consider the process the Lord allowed Nebuchadnezzar to walk through. Once brought low by God, he was brought back to his kingdom. A king once again.

What does this teach us about God's character?

A pastor and author whom I love and respect wrote a series of poems about King Neb that I think are a perfect way to work through the end of our time this week. Reflect on this quote from John Piper.

"To you, O God of grace, I bow,
And by your mercy I do vow,
O God, from this day forth to give
You thanks, and by the way I live,
To say with all my heart I love
You, and I stand amazed that though
I tried to burn your saints, I owe
Them now my soul. And shall I boast
In anything but grace? Foremost
Of all my boasts and thanks is not
That I was king or pow'r my lot,
Or led the nations with a hook,
Or plundered Israel, or took
Your people in captivity,
But that by this you captured me."[2]

What a beautiful, creative poem about an incredible moment in the history of Scripture. A cruel king singing praises to God. A God he questioned. A God he hated. A God whose people he tried to kill. And now the God he believed in to be his Savior.

Restoration. Redemption. It was possible, by God's grace, for this broken king. And sweet one, it is possible for you. No matter how far away you feel. No matter the baggage you carry. No matter how long you feel you've been running. It's not too far. It's not too much. It's not too late. Point your eyes to heaven.

SECTION 4: RESPOND

Daniel didn't get to choose who he had influence over. In fact, Daniel didn't really choose anything about his world. Other than choosing who he would be obedient to—his God, the one true King.

I imagine that as a young boy, Daniel never dreamed he would one day be placed in the center of a metropolis with influence over not one, but three kings.

But God knew. God planned it. Before Daniel was in his mother's womb, God had a plan for him to be the man he would use to influence a nation of people. For the sake of bringing glory to God.

Daniel was placed in a certain city, in a specific time in history for a reason. He was surrounded by kings, eunuchs, and wise men, and God willed for Daniel to influence them all.

Take a moment to think about where you are. Let's break this down together.

Where do you live? What year is it?

Who are you surrounded by?

Who do you encounter on a daily basis?

Think about who you park next to at school. Who sits to your left in math class? Who is always at the gas station at the same time as you? Who is in your small group? Who lives in the same house as you?

Who is in your direct circle of influence? Be specific.

Now I want you to go back through each of the names you listed and think of some specific ways you can point them to Jesus. Think about what you have in common and what interests or hobbies you share to start the conversation.

How can you influence them through their encounters with you?

We are either pointing people to Jesus with our lives, or we are missing chances to do so. You are right where you are at this point in history for a specific purpose only you can fill! This is an incredible role you get to play in God's kingdom. A vessel of the gospel. An influencer for the sake of Christ.

You can change the world by influencing those God has placed in your midst.

I want you to end this week by writing out a prayer here or in your journal. Pray that God would help you clearly see your circle of influence. Ask for wisdom in how to best point these people to the things of Jesus. And surrender yourself to His will. Even when we don't understand or know how, God knows. God sees. And He has you right where you are today for the sake of pointing people to Him.

no filter

Why is truth important?

There is a man in your kingdom who has a _____ of the _____ _____ in him. **Daniel 5:11b**

How would you feel if you were Daniel and it was up to you to speak truth to another difficult king?

When have you had to speak truth to a friend?

When has a friend had to speak truth to you?

Daniel is being called to be a _____ _____ in the midst of a kingdom of sorcerers and magicians and false truth. He is the vessel of the _____.

Use the space provided to note any Scripture references or comments from the video you want to remember.

let's talk

Session five. I do not want to think about the fact that we only have two group sessions together after this. I may or may not be pouting—maybe I will make this study twenty chapters long. (I didn't.) I am so proud of you for continuing to push through and dig deeper and deeper into the Book of Daniel.

Can I take a moment to remind you that our mighty God breathed these words of Scripture into existence many years ago to impact and shape us today? Mind. Blowing. There is truth for you in these words.

Speaking of truth. Let's play a game titled: Amy Byrd Truth Trivia.

Two of each of the three statements below are true. One is false.

1. Amy listens to Christmas music all year long.

2. Amy gets tan in the summer.

3. Amy cannot stand the feel of denim.

1. Amy speaks French.

2. Amy reads cookbooks for fun.

3. Amy hates the word "moist."

1. Amy dreams of being a storm chaser with a cool van.

2. Amy's favorite place in the world is London.

3. Amy has been skydiving three times.

Wasn't that fun?

FYI: I made my husband take the quiz and he got a perfect score which is good news.

Don't judge my answers. Everybody has words they hate and dreams of chasing tornadoes through fields in a van. Right?

In our world today, it is difficult to understand the difference between truth and lies. To know what we can believe. We may struggle to know who to trust. It may be difficult to identify what is real in the midst of the fake.

Think about it for a moment. Standing in line at the grocery store, you are surrounded by magazine after magazine filled with half-truths, embellishments, and rumors. Celebrities who might have broken up. Athletes who might have said something false. Rumors that 99.9 percent of the time are not true.

And social media. Don't get me started. Social media is filled with people who are filtering their lives in such a way so others cannot see the truth. Photos are staged perfectly. Blemishes are hidden and edited away. People hide their truth under filter after filter. We are afraid to let people know who we really are.

Let me explain this another way. Have I mentioned to you how obsessed I am with all things cooking and baking? My recent show I have been watching non-stop is called the "British Baking Championship." Twelve home bakers in a tent are given challenges to bake week after week. They are assigned to make elaborate cakes, incredible chocolates, and even build large structures out of desserts. It is amazing to see what these men and women can do in the kitchen.

Believe it or not, one of the hardest challenges they face is to bake croissants. Simple croissants. Why is that? While croissants are simple and classic, there is a lot of room for error. From the outside, the croissant may look perfect and professionally done. But it isn't until you cut into the inside that you know whether or not it has been properly baked. An expert must examine the core before they can know the quality of the pastry.

From the outside, we might look really good to the world. The first couple of layers may actually be okay. But it takes getting to the core of our hearts to know the truth. Only the One who knows our hearts inside and out, Jesus, knows who we truly are. There is no filter we can use to hide who we are from God. No layers for us to hide underneath. He knows the truth about each of us.

Take a moment to discuss what truth means. Is it difficult for you to trust people? Is it difficult to find the truth in the voices of our culture? Politicians. Leaders. Teachers. Celebrities. Is it difficult for you to let people know the truth about you?

You may be wondering if it's even possible to know the truth. Does the truth change as our lives change? Sisters, the only place truth can be found is in the person of Jesus. And that truth is the same yesterday, today, and forever.

> Jesus told him, "I am the way, the truth, and the life. No one comes to the Father except through me." **John 14:6**

I want the theme of this week to be *no filter*. Let's remove the layers of falsehood we are hiding behind. Let's get down to what is real. Let's get to the truth.

CHARACTER STUDY: KING BELSHAZZAR

Meet the new king of Babylon. In chapter 5, verse 2, it says he is the son of King Neb, but he was not literally the son of Nebuchadnezzar. The word *father* in Aramaic can mean ancestor or predecessor.[1] King Belshazzar wanted his connection to the powerful king of Babylon, King Neb, to be known.[2] King Belshazzar would be the final king of the Babylonian monarchy before it would be captured by Cyrus the Persian in 539 BC.

Just to clarify any possible confusion:
- King Belshazzar—king of Babylon
- Belteshazzar—Daniel's Babylonian name

Daniel was put in a position where he had to decipher the truth from the lies of the culture around him, and then he chose to live by that truth.

Take a moment to list all Daniel has experienced so far in our study.

Taken from home. Living in exile in the midst of a dark culture. Under the reign of a turbulent leader. Given position by the king. And here we find him serving under the reign of a new king of Babylon. Now I want you to spend some time digging in and reading chapter 5 in full.

Remember, all of Scripture is true. I am saying this because the passage we are in this week is...interesting. Full of things to study. And like one of my girls said, "super weird."

We find ourselves at a feast being hosted by the new king of Babylon, King Belshazzar.

Circle the following words that describe the feast:

Dull   Extravagant   Luxurious   Small

Boring   Fancy   Cheap   Expensive

We will dig deep into the details in our personal study, but today in group time I want to build a broad view of this scene and focus on a few key truths.

Who was in attendance at this feast?

The king began to flaunt the things that were in his care—the vessels of gold that were taken out of the temple in Jerusalem—and he began to praise the gods of gold, silver, bronze, iron, wood, and stone. This was an idols feast. People worshiping other gods and doing all they could to be pleased by earthly things.

Does this sound familiar to you? Compare this to the way we saw King Nebuchadnezzar live his early days as king.

So we have idol worship among a group the king has gathered, and we see the Lord show up in a mighty way.

Take a moment to sketch or draw what Scripture describes.

Obviously this message delivered on the walls of the palace troubled the new king. Who did he ultimately seek out to interpret the dream? Daniel. The man the mighty King Nebuchadnezzar had appointed as the chief over his wise men. Because Daniel was special and powerful? No. But because Daniel was known for truth that came from the one true God.

I want you to see, girls, that no matter the king or the circumstance, everyone ultimately seeks answers.

CHALLENGE & GOOD NEWS

Everyone ultimately seeks answers. In times of struggle. In times of loss. We will encounter broken and lost people. And here is the good news: In Jesus, we have the answers to all they seek! How incredible is it that we get to be vessels of the gospel in the lives of those seeking answers! And as King Belshazzar learned, truth is only found in the things of God. No matter how hard we search. Regardless of the number of wise men we may seek, ultimate truth is only found when we first seek Christ.

Take a moment to discuss some "wise men" we may turn to for wisdom rather than to God. Some who come to mind for me would be trusted adults, counselors, or even close friends.

Wisdom and truth will only be found from and in those who seek truth in Jesus. Period. Not only was Daniel filled with wisdom and truth by God, but he was also called to speak the truth in love. As we see in this passage, Daniel was given a dark message to deliver to the king—a difficult truth to communicate to a king he did not know.

Can you imagine how difficult it must have been for Daniel? Explain.

Describe a difficult moment when you had to speak the truth in love.

When have you felt burdened to speak the truth, but chose not to in order to keep the peace or avoid drama? Consider sharing your example with the group.

We must speak the truth no matter the circumstances. Daniel easily could have told the king he did not know what the message on the walls meant. He could have hidden the truth God had given him to communicate. He could have run from the truth. But instead, Daniel chose to speak the truth in love no matter the circumstances.

What does speaking the truth in love mean? It means gentle. Humble in speech. Caring about the heart of the person we are speaking to. Realizing it's ultimately about bringing reconciliation between that person and God.

The same is true for us. As believers we are called to speak the truth—to live out the truth— no matter the circumstances. We are going to dig into what it means to live out the truth, just like Daniel, in our continued study this week. Meet me there, okay?

In your group, discuss the following:

What areas of your life are you filtering?

Are you hiding yourself from people at church or school? From your family or your best friends?

Do you struggle to speak the truth in some circumstances?

HERE & NOW

Social media is a huge part of our world. And that is not a bad thing! Social media becomes an issue only we when we choose to use it poorly. Meaning to get attention, to hurt others, or to twist reality to look better or worse than it is.

Take a moment to list some reasons you post on social media.

What do you hope to gain from your social media posts?

What do you hope people will think of you after seeing your social media posts?

This week I would love for each of our social media accounts to be an encouragement and communicator of truth to those who follow us. This could be fun! Join me? Let's go this week without a filter! I mean it. Let's put up true posts. Nothing altered. Nothing hidden.

FOUR DAY SOCIAL MEDIA CHALLENGE

1. Share one truth of Scripture.

2. Share a story about a true friend.

3. Share a post of your true life (your messy locker, an unmade bed, and so on).

4. Share a post about a truth speaker in your life.

Have I mentioned no filters? No perfect set-ups. Just reality. Just truth. I hope this will help us identify the areas of our lives we filter—from selfies to setting up the perfect picture of our coffee. Truth is always best!

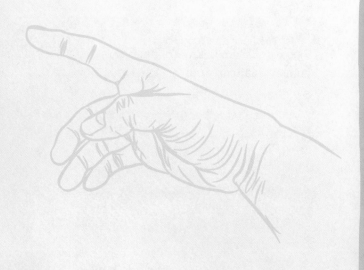

personal study

SECTION 1: KNOWN FOR TRUTH
Daniel 5:10-12

I mentioned to you that I love food. And cooking. And baking. I love to watch people cook. I love to read about people who cook. I love to read recipes teaching me how to cook. I love to feed people. I love to eat. Food is my favorite. It is an outlet for me to be creative and accomplish something tangible.

Plus, pies are delicious. Right? Right.

One of the best compliments I can receive is when someone praises food I have made. I love it when I am at a party or social function and someone gets excited about the dish I brought. At my office, one of the items people like for me to bake are blueberry muffins. Nothing fancy—but they love them. And I love to make them because they make my people happy!

I am known for making blueberry muffins. I am known for other things as well. Telling bad jokes. Loving being around people. Being a bit awkward. Having a loud laugh.

What about you? What are some things you are known for?

Now take a moment to think about some things Daniel was known for. The one trait I want to focus on today when it comes to Daniel is that he was known for interpreting and speaking the truth.

> **10** Because of the outcry of the king and his nobles, the queen came to the banquet hall. "May the king live forever," she said. "Don't let your thoughts terrify you or your face be pale. **11** There is a man in your kingdom who has a spirit of the holy gods in him. In the days of your predecessor he was found to have insight, intelligence, and wisdom like the wisdom of the gods. Your predecessor, King Nebuchadnezzar, appointed him chief of the magicians, mediums, Chaldeans, and diviners. Your own predecessor, the king, **12** did this because Daniel, the one the king named Belteshazzar, was found to have an extraordinary spirit, knowledge and intelligence, and the ability to interpret dreams, explain riddles, and solve problems. Therefore, summon Daniel, and he will give the interpretation." **Daniel 5:10-12**

Circle the phrase from the passage that tells us who Daniel is.

How did the queen describe him to King Belshazzar? And what did the queen say he was able to do?

This is incredible to me! A brand new king. A new situation that befuddled all of the wise men in the kingdom. Yet again, Daniel, the man who was brought to Babylon as a prisoner, was called to the king's court.

Why Daniel? Because this was God's assignment for him. And his assignment was to live faithfully in exile and complete each task presented to him in a way that honored God.

God showed His power through Daniel time and time again during the reign of King Nebuchadnezzar. He even named Daniel the chief of his wise men because the spirit of God lived within him, which enabled him to do miraculous things. Daniel was known for truth—and for speaking it no matter the cost.

When people hear your name, what do you hope comes to their minds? When they see you walk into the room, what do you hope they think?

Are you known for making much of Jesus with your life? Are you known for living out the truth of God's Word every day?

Or are you known for some less healthy things? For being critical? Mean? Whiny? Judgmental? Prideful?

Daniel was known for truth because the truth lived inside him. Living and active in his life. When we surrender our lives to God, the Holy Spirit moves into our hearts. He dwells within us!

Is the presence of God in your life changing the way you live? The things you are known for? Explain.

Consider this quote from Matt Chandler in *Creature of the Word: The Jesus-Centered Church* before you continue in your personal study. Think about the ways God may be calling you to leadership.

"God ultimately raises up leaders for one primary reason: His glory. He shows His power in our weakness. He demonstrates His wisdom in our folly. We are all like a turtle on a fence post. If you walk by a fence post and see a turtle on top of it, then you know someone came by and put it there. In the same way, God gives leadership according to His good pleasure."[3]

SECTION 2: KING BELSHAZZAR
Daniel 5:18-24

God taught King Neb some really big and difficult lessons. He faced nightmares and fear. He was called to humble himself or be humbled. Do you remember where he ended up after he refused to heed the warnings God sent through his dreams?

He ended up losing the reign of his kingdom and living among the animals. The Lord called him to do something, and in his pride he ignored that command. And God took his kingdom away in an instant. God keeps His promises, and King Neb learned that the hard way.

What was the new king's name?

Once again Babylon was under the reign of a king who wanted to make much of himself. He had everything he could possibly desire from a worldly standpoint. The most beautiful palace. A thriving kingdom. Riches. Lavish foods. Surrounded by people who worshiped him and followed his commands. King Belshazzar was living the king's dream. He knew the stories of the king before him, yet he did not let any of the lessons King Neb learned impact his life or world in any way.

In verses 18-20, Daniel contrasted Belshazzar with Nebuchadnezzar.

18 "Your Majesty, the Most High God gave sovereignty, greatness, glory, and majesty to your predecessor Nebuchadnezzar. **19** Because of the greatness he gave him, all peoples, nations, and languages were terrified and fearful of him. He killed anyone he wanted and kept alive anyone he wanted; he exalted anyone he wanted and humbled anyone he wanted. **20** But when his heart was exalted and his spirit became arrogant, he was deposed from his royal throne and his glory was taken from him."

Daniel was saying, "Look! Look at what became of Nebuchadnezzar when he ignored the word of the Lord. Look at how the Lord keeps His promises. Look at what it takes to be a king who honors the one true God." Daniel delivered truth into the heart of another king. And that truth should have shaken him.

That's what the truth does. It teaches us. It changes us.

Daniel shared the truth with King Belshazzar. A truth that was calling him to change his life. I would imagine truth of such magnitude might frighten the king. Might even cause him to consider change. Later on, we will dig deeper and examine how the king responded to the truth Daniel shared.

Can you think of a time when you were confronted with an uncomfortable truth? How did you respond?

Alternatively, when have you confronted someone else with a hard truth? How did that go?

Truth is not always easy to hear or to share, but the truth of God's Word is the only place we can firmly stand and trust.

SECTION 3: NOT EVERYONE WILL RESPOND TO TRUTH
Daniel 5:25-28

Daniel warned King Belshazzar. He told him the stories of King Nebuchadnezzar when choosing to ignore God's commands. He reminded him of the hurt and the loss.

How did Belshazzar respond? Did he, like King Neb, humble himself before God?

No. In fact, Belshazzar did the complete opposite. He lifted himself up. Raised his glass to fake gods. Used the sacred vessels from the temple in Jerusalem.

Take a moment to either write out a description or draw a picture of this feast we see in Daniel chapter 5.

Belshazzar! Do you not see you are headed for ruin? Do you not see that God does not share affection and attention? Have you forgotten the last king who lived in your palace ended up living with pigs because of his idol worship?

This is what Daniel tried to do. He spoke a word from God that included a warning of the grave news about the future for him and his kingdom.

Part of the way God revealed Himself to Belshazzar was with handwriting on the wall. I know the interpretation of the handwriting may be a bit confusing. So let's spend some time looking at the details.

Read Daniel 5:25.

In the boxes below, write out the four words that were inscribed by the hand.

Now read verses 26-28 and write in each of the specific boxes what these words meant, according to Daniel's interpretation.

The words Daniel read and interpreted were Aramaic. Read as verbs in Aramaic, these words read: *Numbered. Numbered. Weighed. Divided.* This meant the Lord had numbered the days of Belshazzar's kingdom because he had been weighed (*Tekel*) in the balance and found wanting.

> What does verse 28 say would happen to the kingdom Belshazzar ruled?

Truth. His days were numbered. He should humble himself before God. Truth was in front of his face, and he chose to ignore it. Daniel couldn't control that. All Daniel could do was present the truth.

The same is true for us. All we can do is place the truth in front of others. Humbly. In obedience. And trust God to be in control of the rest.

This can be difficult for us. We may have friends we so desperately want to know Jesus. We want them to see His love for them. We want them to stop their sin and surrender to Jesus.

Sister, all we can do is present them with the truth. Show them Jesus. And let God do the rest.

> List some people in your life you want to understand the truth.

SECTION 4: RESPOND

I want us today to claim the truth. This is a big journaling day for us. I want you to write out five truths about God.

Who He is. What He has done for us. What He has called us to do. And so on.

Then I want you to journal some very specific and tangible ways you can apply these to your life today. I will give you a personal example:

> I believe God's timing is perfect.
> I need to put this truth into action in my life by not trying to rush having answers to all of my questions. I want to understand why my dad is so sick and when he will be well. I want dates. I want details. I want to know when he will be back to normal. God is calling me to trust Him in this season of waiting. God is calling me to trust His timing is best and His timing is perfect.

Your turn! Make it personal. Five truths and then apply them.

_____

_____

_____

_____

_____

_____

_____

_____

_____

_____

_____

_____

run to Him

Why do you think the other administrators and satraps were upset when Daniel was promoted to a higher position?

What fault did the other administrators and satraps find in Daniel?

Why is obedience scary? Why is obedience hard?

May your God, whom you _____ _____, rescue you!
Daniel 6:16b

What was King Darius' response to finding Daniel unharmed in the lions' den?

We are all going to be called to walk in _____.

When have you had to be obedient even when it was scary?

Use the space provided to note any Scripture references or comments from the video you want to remember.

let's talk

It thrills my heart to know you have continued to press forward in seeking God through the reading of His Word.

> On a scale of one to ten, how committed have you been to our group session content and personal study pages?
>
> 1 · 10
> I have not completed a single session.   I have been a rockstar!

Let's have a pep talk. I understand how busy life can be. We recently had our first baby boy and I have learned a life lesson that I wish I had known sooner—nap when you can. Sisters, seasons are always going to be busy. Yes, some more than others. But there will always be something you can put before your time committed to studying God's Word. I want to encourage you to really dig in this week. Listen. Engage. Invest. God's Word is alive and active! It will transform your life today. I am praying it does just that.

I want you to take some time before we dive into our passage today to just quiet your hearts as a group. Pray the Lord would move during your group time and continue to do so as you move into your personal study.

I believe that many of you will be familiar with the portion of Scripture we are reading today. Daniel in the lions' den. Some of you have grown up hearing this story. You have seen it on videos and done coloring sheets of Daniel with a big, furry lion and perhaps even acted it out in Sunday school.

My hope is today the words of this passage will become more alive than ever before. Because you have come to know Daniel. You are fully aware his journey in obedience to God began long before the lions' den.

In chapter 6, Daniel was, yet again, forced to choose between being obedient to the command of the king of Babylon or to the one true King—our God.

> Take a moment in your group to discuss when you have had to be obedient. What are the consequences of being disobedient?

I'm guessing a lot of you mentioned keeping your rooms clean, being home on time, and not using all of your data in the first five minutes of the month. (I am smirking because I live my life surrounded by girls who use up their data in the first five minutes of the month.)

And it is my assumption that, for many of you, the consequences of disobedience involve an earlier curfew, limited social activities, and no data at all.

Each of us has a gauge of obedience we can picture in our minds. So did Daniel. His unwillingness to disobey God had earthly consequences that far outweighed those we mentioned in our light-hearted examples above.

Let's gear up and dive into chapter 6.

Ask someone in your group to read the 28 verses aloud.

Does this story sound familiar? We are introduced to a new king of Babylon in this passage. We first knew King Nebuchadnezzar. Then, for a short time we had King Belshazzar. Now enters King Darius from Media who came to trust in God for his salvation. We begin chapter 6 learning more about the hierarchy Darius set up over the kingdom. (FYI: Satraps were administrators that served under the king.)

Take a moment to list those who were involved in his leadership as seen in verses 1-3.

There is quite a power struggle going on in this passage. Daniel, because of his character, has proven to be the most capable and trustworthy among all of the governors and satraps appointed by the king. These leaders did not respond well to this, and they came up with a plan to derail Daniel from his success. A jealous plot.

Can you think of another point in the Book of Daniel when disobedience to kingdom law was reported to a king?

In verses 6-9, we begin to see their plan take shape.

6 Then these high officials and satraps came by agreement to the king and said to him, "O King Darius, live forever! **7** All the high officials of the kingdom, the prefects and the satraps, the counselors and the governors are agreed that the king should establish an ordinance and enforce an injunction, that whoever makes petition to any god or man for thirty days, except to you, O king, shall be cast into the den of lions. **8** Now, O king, establish the injunction and sign the document, so that it cannot be changed, according to the law of the Medes and the Persians, which cannot be revoked." **9** Therefore King Darius signed the document and injunction. **Daniel 6:6-9 (ESV)**

Circle the ordinance these men convinced the king to put into place.

Underline the consequences of disobeying the ordinance.

Highlight the phrase "except to you, O king" in verse 7.

These men were attempting to get to the king in a personal way. Maliciously and intentionally, they were toying with the king's affections and hoping he would want to be worshiped among the gods as the past kings of Babylon did. And all of this—the audience with the king, the ordinance and every effort—was to persecute Daniel.

Like Daniel, we will face persecution. Sister, the more we look like God, the less we will look like this world. We are going to look different and live different. The ways we respond. The ways we love. The ways we speak. All of these things will cause us to stand out as different from the rest of the world. And being different will at times cause others to treat us poorly. To try to hurt us. To exclude us. To talk about us. To try to harm us.

Persecution is lived out in different ways all over the world. Daniel's response to persecution was to seek God. Verses 10-13 are powerful. The ordinance was made known to Daniel and we see his reaction to this law.

What did Daniel do in response to the ordinance?

Daniel sought God. He went to his home and bowed before his true King. I want to make this very real for us girls. Consistently, we see Daniel seek God in times of trial. We see him ask God for boldness and strength to be obedient to God, no matter the cost.

This awakens my heart. It causes me to stop and consider what I might do if I encountered this same situation. My first shot at it? I would go somewhere and hide from those who sought to harm me. And never ever come out again.

But here we see Daniel go *home* and seek God. He didn't hide. He didn't run. He bowed. With faith. In obedience. Trusting in the perfect plan of his God. And ultimately, we see in verses 10-17 that God's perfect plan was for Daniel to be thrown into a den of lions. We will dig into this more in our personal study this week.

Discuss for a moment how you respond to tough situations.

Where do you run? To whom do you run?

How would you have felt if God's plan for your life was to send you into a den of lions?

Our obedience changes others. I am amazed at how emotionally invested King Darius was in Daniel's life. Daniel was a man the king trusted and thought much of. Daniel was one of his guys, his chosen few. Yet King Darius signed an ordinance that ultimately sent his guy to the lions' den. Even as king, he could not do anything to stop it.

In the last portion of this passage, Darius fasted, struggled with sleep, and went early to check on Daniel after his time in the lions' den. After seeing what God had done for Daniel, Darius honored God and praised Him for His steadfast love.

Incredible! Daniel was not the one who saved Darius. The one true God saved his soul. But through Daniel's obedience, God revealed himself to King Darius. In the same way, our obedience to God and the way we live our lives can have an impact on the lives of others!

We are vessels of the gospel of Jesus Christ. We are bearers of the good news. You can change the world when you live differently. Love differently. Look differently. God will use your life to change the lives of others—all for His glory.

Take some time to examine your heart and answer these questions honestly before you close your book today.

How does God call you to be obedient? List the ways here.

What are some ways living in obedience to God will change how you live your life?

How have you seen God honor your obedience?

What are the consequences of disobedience?

HERE & NOW

I have the opportunity to travel with my students all over the country each year on mission trips. It is one of the greatest joys of my life! In the summer of 2016, we traveled to Chicago to serve with local churches and spend time in the city. One of my favorite assignments was spending time in public parks simply engaging people in conversation and prayerfully having an opportunity to share the gospel with them. I had a team of seven students I partnered with on this particular day, and we were stationed at The Bean in the middle of downtown Chicago. This is where I met my friend Sue. She was an interior designer, lived in a fancy loft, and was engaged to a man she said she loved with all of her heart.

Sue and I entered into a conversation that I will never forget. She showed great interest in the stories of the Bible and the "God you say is alive" as she put it. By God's grace, I had the chance to talk with Sue about God and His great love for her. She made it clear she had some major hesitations, but she felt God was calling her to surrender her life to Him. I prayed with Sue, gave her my information and information on a local church, and walked away begging God to continue a work in her life.

Two months later I received a text from Sue. It read "Amy. It is Sue from Chicago. I hope that you remember me. I wanted you to know that we are now sisters in God's kingdom. I asked God to take over my heart one month after we met in the park and life has been a bit crazy since. I joined a church and they are teaching me to walk with God and what it means to change my life to bring Him glory. I did endure some heartbreak in this process. My fiancé found out about my decision to follow Christ, and he broke up with me. He will not speak to me. His family will not speak to me. It hurts. But my God is teaching me He will heal me. I will never forget our talk and how God used you from Alabama to talk to me. Thank you."

Sue lost her fiancé. He wouldn't even speak to her. And her response?

God will heal.

She chose to trust God and continue to walk forward in obedience. I will never forget Sue and will never stop praising our God for the work He did in her life and in mine.

SECTION 1: LIFETIME OF OBEDIENCE
Daniel 6:1-10

You guys. I just want to give Daniel a hug. A hug, a piece of cake, and a safe place that doesn't involve any dreams or dysfunctional kings or lions. No lions. When I take one giant step back and look at the big picture of what we have seen in the Book of Daniel, one word comes to mind: *Obedient*.

Daniel was obedient. Shadrach, Meshach, and Abednego were obedient. To God alone. No matter the cost.

Let's refresh our memory.

> How did Daniel and his three friends respond when they were told to eat certain foods and drinks when they arrived in Babylon?

> What happened when Shadrach, Meshach, and Abednego were obedient to God and refused to bow to the image of gold that King Nebuchadnezzar built?

They didn't eat the food. They didn't bow to the image of gold. And Daniel, who was over 80 years old at the time, was commanded to bow once again.

> To whom was Daniel commanded to worship in the first verses of chapter 6?

> When Daniel learned that the document had been signed, he went into his house. The windows in its upstairs room opened toward Jerusalem, and three times a day he got down on his knees, prayed, and gave thanks to his God, just as he had done before. **Daniel 6:10**

This is really powerful. Once again Daniel was faced with a decision.

In the space below, either draw or write out the scene we see played out in verse 10.

His life was in danger. He knew what was to come if he didn't obey the ordinance from the king. Yet, he chose to bow only to the true King. Why? Because he refused to worship anything or anyone other than the one true God. No king could persuade him. No threat could convince him. He was devoted to God. For life. In the details of every day.

I love how Daniel is described earlier in this passage. Write out Daniel 6:3.

Circle the words "extraordinary spirit." Some translations say "an excellent spirit."

I have mentioned several times now that living a life pleasing to God will cause us to look different. And gracious, did Daniel stand out among the men in Babylon! So much so that men had to be malicious in setting him up to fail.

The king loved Daniel. He was one of his favorites. He was given influence and power. Because he was so great? No. But because he was obedient to his great God.

This is an interesting thing for me to consider. What does it look like to live a life of obedience to God—in every detail of my every day? How can I, like Daniel and his three friends, honor God and show my obedience to Him in the small and large things of my life? Scripture is our road map for such a question.

First, in the way I begin my day.

12 Therefore, as God's chosen ones, holy and dearly loved, put on compassion, kindness, humility, gentleness, and patience, **13** bearing with one another and forgiving one another if anyone has a grievance against another. Just as the Lord has forgiven you, so you are also to forgive. **Colossians 3:12-13**

Do you start your day without acknowledging your need for God?

Do you start your day only thinking of yourself?

In the way I treat others.

Do nothing out of selfish ambition or conceit, but in humility consider others as more important than yourselves. **Philippians 2:3**

Do you treat other girls poorly because of jealousy or division?

Do you put the needs of others before you own needs?

Do you handle conflict in a way that honors God?

In the way I dress.

19 Don't you know that your body is a temple of the Holy Spirit who is in you, whom you have from God? You are not your own, **20** for you were bought at a price. So glorify God with your body. **1 Corinthians 6:19-20**

Who are you trying to please when you dress yourself?

What do your clothes communicate to people about you?

Do your clothes cause people to stumble?

In the way I speak.

Her mouth speaks wisdom, and loving instruction is on her tongue. **Proverbs 31:26**

How do you speak to people when you are upset or frustrated?

Do you show kindness to others even if they are different than you?

Do you gossip and repeat stories?

In the way I work.

Commit your way to the Lord; trust in him, and he will act. Psalm 37:5

Do you accomplish tasks to the best of your ability or just enough to get by?

Are you working hard to gain acclaim for yourself or for the glory of God?

Do you see your everyday tasks as opportunities to honor God? Explain.

Sister, I am not just encouraging you to a lifetime of obedience. I am telling you it is your calling! Man's end goal is to glorify God and enjoy Him forever.

What is standing in between you and a lifetime of obedience?

In what areas of your life are you showing disobedience?

End this time journaling and writing out ways you, like Daniel, can live a life of obedience to God. In all things, big and small.

SECTION 2: OBEDIENCE HAS A COST
Daniel 6:11-16

I wish I could tell you that your obedience to God will win you a lifetime of chocolate cake, a crown, and lots of time at the pool. Doesn't sound lovely? That's just not the case.

Obedience to God does not equal an easy life. Obedience to God does not mean life will be simple. Obedience to God does not assure you will never go through seasons of hurt. I actually feel comfortable telling you obedience to God will make your life here on earth more complicated, difficult, and sometimes painful.

But God does not call you to live life alone. He has gone before you. He stands with you. He keeps you safe.

> Haven't I commanded you: be strong and courageous? Do not be afraid or discouraged, for the LORD your God is with you wherever you go. **Joshua 1:9**

Sister, life here is difficult and painful because we live in a really dark and broken world. A world that wants us to look and act a certain way. A world that is *nothing* like the home we were created for. So living a life that is obedient to God is going to make our time here in our temporary assignment rather difficult. Because we are in a battle against the things of this world. And battles are exhausting and difficult.

But, the great news? We are in a battle in which we are already sure of our victory. God won. The devil was defeated. So we do not have to be afraid. Certainly we will face trials and hurts that cause us to feel fear at times. We will cry. We will ask questions. We will shake in our boots. But we will not be defeated or consumed.

Daniel knew this to be true. He knew obedience had a cost. But he continued to walk forward in obedience. Right into a den of lions.

Refresh your memory—go back and read Daniel 6:6-9 again. Daniel was commanded to bow down and worship King Darius because of an ordinance the malicious men in the king's court had convinced him to sign. There was nothing Darius could do after he signed the edict.

When have you felt like you were being thrown into a lions' den?

What difficult moments have you faced as a consequence of your obedience to God?

Did you lose something or did you have to face a fear in the midst of that obedience?

Sister, I don't know your story. I do not know the trials you are facing. I do not know the mountain you are climbing right now. But I do know there is a God in heaven who adores you and who is walking with you. And that God is alive and active and worthy of your whole life. Trust Him. Follow Him. You might be in a battle or in a lions' den, but you will not be consumed.

Now let's read one of my favorite passages of the entire Book of Daniel. The king went to the lions' den to check on Daniel the morning after he was thrown in.

What does the king ask Daniel in verse 20?

Try to imagine yourself in this moment. The king was heartbroken to send Daniel to the lions' den. And now, in the quiet of the early morning, the king stood outside the den and asked Daniel if he had been rescued.

Gracious, that makes my heart beat faster! I imagine a moment of silence before...

> **21** Then Daniel spoke with the king: "May the king live forever. **22** My God sent his angel and shut the lions' mouths; and they haven't harmed me, for I was found innocent before him. And also before you, Your Majesty, I have not done harm." **Daniel 6:21-22**

FAST FACT: In this miracle, there is speculation the angel was the same as the fourth person who showed up in the fiery furnace with Shadrach, Meshach, and Abednego.

This makes me want to scream! In all the best ways. No harm was done. Why? Because he was _____ _____ before _____.

My friend, you may face a battle in your life of obedience to God. You may hurt. Your body may be physically sick. You may lose someone. You may be lonely. You may be afraid. But God will shut the mouths of those who seek to hurt you. He will guard you. No harm will be done to you.

Please don't hear me say we will never suffer great loss. Yes, God did spare Daniel's life. God openly honored Daniel's faith for the purpose of showing His glory to those in Babylon. But there are times when God's will is for our earthly lives to be lost.

God may be bringing glory to Himself by allowing one of His children to be delivered and have victory in losing our life. That is a difficult truth. A cost of obedience and a life lived for God. I do not say this lightly—that is not a loss. We have victory in our God. And no battle can take that away.

Are you in a lions' den? Are you facing the battle of your life? Explain.

SECTION 3: DARIUS RESPONDS
Daniel 6:17-27

King Darius. Bless him. The man was fooled by men under his leadership to sign an edict commanding all men to worship him for 30 days. Little did he know, these men had a plan. They were out to get Daniel and put his ever-growing influence and success to an end.

I must say I was surprised to see the emotional response the king had once he found out Daniel would suffer the consequences of the edict he had signed.

> **13** Then they replied to the king, "Daniel, one of the Judean exiles, has ignored you, the king, and the edict you signed, for he prays three times a day." **14** As soon as the king heard this, he was very displeased; he set his mind on rescuing Daniel and made every effort until sundown to deliver him. **Daniel 6:13-14**

Remember Darius was the man who gave Daniel, who was over the age of 80, such influence and power in the first place. He loved Daniel. He trusted Daniel. And now, without realizing it, he had sentenced Daniel to be thrown into the lions' den. Unfortunately, the king could not take back his ordinance. According to the Medo-persian law, this could not be changed. Even by the king.[1]

So, Daniel was thrown into the lions' den.

Write out what Darius said to Daniel in verse 16.

Note at the time, Darius refers to God as Daniel's God. This shows us Darius had not yet surrendered his life to the one true God. But I do believe that in this passage of Scripture, we are seeing Darius' heart searching for a savior. God is at work in his life. And I believe God allowed Daniel to go into the lions' den so it might impact the life of this king.

Darius couldn't sleep. He did not eat. His spirit was troubled that Daniel, an innocent man, was in a den of lions due to his edict. At dawn's light, the king rushed to the lions' den and found Daniel to be unharmed. God used this trial in the life of Daniel to bring Darius to a place of surrender. And surrender to God he did!

> **25** "Then King Darius wrote to those of every people, nation, and language who live on the whole earth: "May your prosperity abound. **26** I issue a decree that in all my royal dominion, people must tremble in fear before the God of Daniel: For he is the living God, and he endures forever; his kingdom will never be destroyed, and his dominion has no end. **27** He rescues and delivers; he performs signs and wonders in the heavens and on the earth, for he has rescued Daniel from the power of the lions." **Daniel 6:25-27**

How incredible! Listen to Darius worshiping the one true King. God used Daniel's obedience to transform the heart and life of a king—all for God's glory!

Who in your life may God be using your story to encourage?

Can you see ways the Lord has used situations you have walked through to draw people to Himself? If so, give some examples.

SECTION 4: HE IS THE HERO

Girls, I want to share with you an excerpt of the *Jesus Storybook Bible*. This is one of my favorite resources and sweet way to read God's Word.

This is author Sally Lloyd-Jones' story of Daniel and the Scary Sleepover (AKA: Daniel in the lions' den). This is one of my favorite resources and a sweet way to read God's Word.

"The king went back to his palace, but he didn't sleep that night. Not a wink. He tossed and turned until finally, at the first glimmer of dawn, he leaped out of bed and ran straight to the den. 'Daniel?' he cried. 'Has your God rescued you?'

'YES!' Daniel shouted. 'God sent an angel to close the lions' mouths!' ... The king brought Daniel out of the den. 'Look!' he said. 'Daniel doesn't even have a scratch.'

The king made a new law: 'Daniel's God is the true God. The God who Rescues! Pray to him instead!'

God would keep on rescuing his people. And the time was coming when God would send another brave Hero, like Daniel, who would love God and do what God said— whatever it cost him, even if it meant he would die. And together they would pull off the Greatest Rescue the world has ever known."[2]

Sister, Daniel followed God in obedience straight into the lions' den. And God rescued him.

What I love about this story from the *Jesus Storybook Bible* is it points us to another rescuer, our Savior. Our hero, Jesus. The One who faced ultimate fear and persecution and worldly trial. The One who gave His life for us. We are called to surrender our lives and follow Him without hesitation.

Jesus. The ultimate picture of obedience. He gave His life for you and for me.

I want you to write out or draw a moment when you have been obedient to God. Highlight how your Rescuer saved you and provided for you in the midst of that moment. Your lions' den.

sovereign over all

As they sought to live a life of _____ and _____, God sustained them. And He was in control of every bit of every minute.

Write a quick summary of what we've studied in each session.

Session 1:

Session2:

Session 3:

Session 4:

Session 5:

Session 6:

Our call is not to look like the things of this world, but to look like _____.

What are some of your milestone moments? Start thinking about what you would include on your own timeline of faith.

Use the space provided to note any Scripture references or comments from the video you want to remember.

let's talk

Here we are. Our final full week of study. If I were with you, I would give each of you a hug and a giant sprinkle donut for making it to the final chapter of this study. (Donuts are my love language.) It really makes me emotional to consider all our hearts have been through in the past six weeks. I hope you are changed. I pray God met you on the pages of His Word and rocked your world.

My prayer is that in the future when you hear someone reference the Book of Daniel, you will know exactly what they are talking about. That you will speak about the stories with the same familiarity as you speak about things like One Direction and current TV shows. You dissected these verses. It is personal to you.

You might wonder why we are having another group session if we aren't going to read another chapter of the Book of Daniel. I get that. Honestly, I asked myself the same question. The truth? We need just one more group session to wrap up and put a bow on all that we have done in the last six weeks.

We have encountered images of gold 90 feet high, furnaces of blazing fire, weird dreams of kings, and a den filled with lions. And throughout all of the passages of Scripture we have studied and all of the kings of Babylon we have been through, we have seen one main theme.

God is sovereign. He has supreme power and authority over all that has happened, is happening, and will happen at all times. God is fully in control of all things. He is all-knowing and all-powerful. He has complete control over every thing. At all times. Across history.

That is a mighty God!

As a group, I want you to spend some time discussing these passages of Scripture which point to God's sovereignty. Write down what each passage teaches us about God's power and control:

> Our God is in heaven and does whatever he pleases. **Psalm 115:3**

> A person's heart plans his way, but the Lord determines his steps.
> **Proverbs 16:9**

He said: LORD, God of our ancestors, are you not the God who is in heaven, and do you not rule over all the kingdoms of the nations? Power and might are in your hand, and no one can stand against you.
2 Chronicles 20:6

What an amazing God we serve! He has a plan for us. He reigns in the heavens and works all things for our good and His glory. He rules over all the kingdoms and nations. Those of the past. Those of the present. Those of the future. No king or ruler can overpower our true King. We certainly found this to be true through the first six chapters of the Book of Daniel. God made it clear He was in control and His power could not be matched.

In what ways did God show His power and control in the life of Daniel?

Daniel 1:8-9

Daniel 1:17

Daniel 2:19

Daniel 5:13-14

Daniel 5:29

Daniel 6:21-23

In what ways did God show His power and control in the life of Shadrach, Meshach, and Abednego?

Daniel 3:16-18

Daniel 3:25-27

Daniel 3:30

In the life of the kings?

Daniel 4:34-37

Daniel 5:30

Throughout Scripture we see the theme of God's ultimate control and authority. He protected. He rescued. He confronted. He punished. He spoke. All for His glory. What a beautiful picture. What a sweet story. Our God who we trust and know is constantly in control. All-knowing. All-powerful. No matter what we face. No matter where we go. No matter how we feel.

> For from him and through him and to him are all things. To him be glory forever. Amen. **Romans 11:36**

Sister, this isn't just the theme in the Book of Daniel. The God who was in control and alive in the Book of Daniel is the very same God in control and alive at this very moment. He always has been. He always will be. And He longs for you to live a life that brings Him glory.

He will not stand by while we worship other gods. He will not share our hearts or our affections. He alone deserves all of our praise and to Him alone shall we bow down. He will not leave us to battle alone. He will be with you always. This is our God! And He has a perfect plan for your life.

I so wish that I could take you by the hand right now and tell you face-to-face how dearly loved you are by your Creator. The one who designed every detail of your life for a specific purpose. The one who knows the number of hairs on your head and who mapped out your days before you were born.

He has created you to be a world changer for His glory! He is not done with you yet. In fact, He is just getting started.

I want to end our time together (literally crying at my dining room table typing that sentence) by creating a timeline for your life. Along the way, we've seen Daniel's timeline of faith. How he trusted. How he was obedient. We know Daniel's story. So now let's map out your story.

First, I'm going to help you out by creating a timeline of my own. Our timelines aren't going to feature large golden idols, but they might feature boyfriends we placed before God. You won't see a den of lions on my timeline, but you will see years of waiting on Baby Byrd. Girls, we may not live in Babylon, but we are still living in a culture that doesn't want to worship the one true God. A world that places pride and arrogance before God. And we are still facing a city of lions that wants us to all look just alike. But we were made to look different. We were made to stand against culture and face those lions, just like Daniel.

Amy's timeline

Age 8
Surrendered my life to Jesus.

Age 6
Became a member of my home church. Started developing knowledge of who God is.

Age 11
Challenged to dive deeper into God's Word in my first discipleship group.

Age 20
Started dating my future husband. Learned to keep Christ first. Saw God's provision after season of hurt.

Age 18
My first and hardest breakup. Sought healing and satisfaction in Jesus.

Age 16
Dark season. Called to test if my faith was real.

Age 22
Married William. Entered a new season of trusting God as husband and wife.

Age 26
Almost lost my dad to cancer. Season of darkness and trusting God in the midst of confusion and fear.

Age 25
Entered into a season of waiting for Baby Byrd. Much sickness and hurt.

Age 27
Our first son, Timothy, was born. Great joy in God's provision!

create your own timeline

leader guide

leader tips

Listed below are some tips to make this an effective and meaningful study for you and your girls.

Pray diligently.
Ask God to prepare you to lead this study. Pray individually and specifically for the girls in your group. Make this a priority in your personal walk and preparation.

Prepare adequately.
Don't just wing this. Take time to preview each session so you have a good grasp of the content. Look over the group session and consider your girls. Feel free to delete or reword the questions provided, and add other questions that fit your group better.

Provide resources.
Each student will need a Bible study book. Try to have extras on hand for girls who join the group later in the study.

Encourage freely.
Cheer for your girls and encourage them to participate in every part of the study.

Lead by example.
Make sure you complete all the personal study. Be willing to share your story, what you're learning, and your questions as you discuss together.

Be aware.
If girls are hesitant to discuss their thoughts and questions in a larger group, consider dividing into smaller groups to provide a setting more conducive to conversation.

Follow up.
If a student mentions a prayer request or need, make sure to follow up. It may be a situation where you can get others in the group involved in helping out.

Evaluate often.
After each session and throughout the study, assess what needs to be changed to more effectively lead the study.

Daniel 1

GET STARTED

Today is important. Your first small group meeting with your girls. Kick off your time today by getting to know your girls and helping them get to know each other.

Middle school groups might enjoy beginning with a few ice breaker games (look on Pinterest for tons of ideas) or playing a name game to help them get to know one another. High school groups might enjoy an opportunity just to introduce themselves, share their names, and a few things everyone should know about them.

I also want to encourage you to create some type of signed discipleship covenant and spend some time walking through this with them. I do these for each of my girls groups every year. It asks them to commit to love each other well, attend group regularly, come to meetings prepared to discuss, and live a life that honors God.

This is a sweet way to set the tone for the study, but also helps them understand that spending time in God's Word is not to be taken lightly. We are growing in the spiritual disciplines by digging into God's Word each week.

PRESS PLAY

Watch the Session One Video (included in the DVD Kit). Allow time for group discussion afterward.

LET'S TALK

Read through the main session and highlight your "must hit" points for group time as you prepare. Be sure to note the following:

- Our culture shapes us and influences us more than we realize. Help girls make this personal. Now is a good time to include examples of specific things that may occur in your town or state that would help them connect with the idea of culture. This is also a good time to mention current events they may be aware of.

- We will dive straight into the first chapter of Daniel this week. Encourage girls to bring their Bibles each week, so they can engage in the passage and interact with it by taking notes or highlighting in their own Bibles.

• This week girls will dive deep into Daniel 1 during their personal study. The passage will cause us to examine our lives, and the fact we were created not for this world but for an eternal home with God forever. This idea might be difficult for your girls to wrap their minds around and potentially could bring up many questions in their hearts. Look for opportunities to have gospel conversations this week. I am praying for the Lord to awaken hearts and draw girls to Himself.

HERE & NOW

End your time today by allowing girls to ask questions about anything in the passage that is unclear to them. Allow this to be a time for girls to discuss and encourage one another as they seek out truth in Scripture. Pray for the Lord to bring your group together in biblical community and that His Word would come alive in their lives as they go throughout their days.

FOLLOW UP

Personal. Study. This is going to be new for some girls. Connect with the girls in your group this week and ask each girl how her personal study is going. This will be a perfect time to encourage the girls in your group and keep them accountable. If you are in a group message with your girls, send out some question prompts to go along with the personal study to engage them mid-week. Example: How would you have felt if you had been taken from your home and exiled to an entirely new city? Would you have been afraid or been able to trust God without fear?

Daniel 2

GET STARTED

Week two! Allow girls some time to debrief you on the week they had. Ask them how they did with their personal study. This is a neat opportunity for the girls in your group to be encouraged and challenged by one another.

Then I would encourage you to partner your girls up in groups of two or three (pairs are ideal). If it isn't awkward, encourage them to connect with someone they don't usually talk to. Once they are in pairs or groups of three, ask them to discuss the following questions:

1. What is the biggest stresser for you right now?

2. What is your favorite thing in the world to do?

3. How can I pray for you right now?

After giving the girls time to move through the questions, instruct them to pray in their groups. Ask girls how that felt. Awkward? Fine? Weird? Normal?

Help them understand it is sometimes difficult to let others in on the details of our lives, but at the same time it is a joy to be known. We were made to live life together and know the details of each others' lives. We were made to pray together in biblical community! Being known and loved by true friends requires vulnerability, but we were made for community. And our community matters.

PRESS PLAY

Watch the Session Two Video (included in the DVD Kit). Allow time for group discussion afterward.

LET'S TALK

It is really important for you to control the conversation today. Do not let the girls chase rabbits or vent about their relationships. Yes—I am asking them to consider their community and, in some cases, I am encouraging them to make some community changes. I am not, however, in support of your group becoming a vent/counseling session. Resist the drama! With that being said, here are some main points to touch on this week:

- Walk girls through Daniel 2 and help them see how Daniel and his friends responded to trials. They came together and they prayed.

- This week may be challenging for some of your girls to be vulnerable or honest as they deal with some discomfort in acknowledging their friendships are not healthy. Remind the girls there is grace, and they are not "in too deep" in unhealthy friendships to be able to make this right. Talk with them about some practical ways they can begin to pull away from unhealthy friendships. This is a good time to connect the relationships King Nebuchadnezzar had. All of the people he surrounded himself with let him down.

- Emphasize we were created for biblical community. Help them see the importance of God-honoring friendships in their lives.

HERE & NOW

Use the end of group time today to give girls some personal reflection time. Ask them to spread out in the room and give them each a blank sheet of paper or encourage them to write in their journals. Give them a white crayon or let them use their finger to write out the initials of someone they are in an unhealthy relationship with. Prompt girls to pray about addressing this relationship this week. Next, have them write out the initials of someone they are in a healthy relationship with. Encourage them to praise God for this friendship and ask that it might grow.

FOLLOW UP

What we have asked the girls to do this week is tough. Dealing with people is messy. Take a moment to either write your girls a note or connect with them individually. Let them know you are praying for them as they seek to honor God in their relationships. Also remind them you are available to talk if they need you. Sister, they will need you.

Daniel 3

GET STARTED

This is one of my favorite weeks of the entire study. We're going to take a look at faith. What it is and how God calls us to live it out. It is really important for us to understand we are saved by grace through faith in a living God!

Write out the word *faith* on a whiteboard, poster board, or somewhere prominent in your meeting space. Start you time together by asking the girls to define *faith* in their own words. Encourage each of them to speak and attempt to verbalize what it means to have faith. Ask several volunteers to share times in their lives when they have had faith or how their faith has been tested.

PRESS PLAY

Watch the Session Three Video (included in the DVD Kit). Allow time for group discussion afterward.

LET'S TALK

Our passage today is one that may be very familiar to some of your girls who have grown up in church. Encourage them to see the story with fresh eyes! Direct them to put themselves in the narrative and consider how they might have responded.

- Walk your girls through Daniel chapter 3. Help them bring this story to life.

- There is an opportunity here to make this story more personal for your girls. Think about where you live and the culture of your town/city. Help them to see some areas where those in your city might be bowing to certain things. For example, I live in a big football town. Everyone goes to the games and loves it. I myself am not a huge football girl, and that makes me very different from most of the people I am surrounded by.

- Note that Shadrach, Meshach, and Abednego were willing to die for the sake of being faithful to God. This was not a fairytale story; it was very dark.

- Each girl's story will be different. Help them identify where they are in putting their faith in Christ and ask a few volunteers to verbalize a time in their lives when they had to show faith in the midst of fear.

HERE & NOW

Although we will most likely not be called to bow to golden images during our lifetime, we all have idols we are facing! End your time by asking girls to identify some idols they are tempted to bow to. Ask them to identify images of gold that have been built before their eyes. Examples: relationships, making the cheerleading squad, being chosen as top of the class. Help them to see how these idols may not be bad, but they become sin when they are placed before our relationship with Christ.

FOLLOW UP

Encourage girls to do something about the idols they addressed in your group time. Whether it was an unhealthy relationship or having the perfect body, remind them the only person or thing worthy of our submission and our adoration is our God! The one true King. Make personal connections and offer to help your girls walk through the process of addressing idols and being faithful to God by putting Him first.

Daniel 4

GET STARTED

Grab some magazines for this week's study. Any with pictures will do. (This goes without saying but make sure there isn't anything inappropriate for your girls in the content.) Bring them to your group meeting and allow girls a few minutes to glance at them before you officially begin your time together. Note the things they say as they work their way through the pages of the magazines. I did this with a group of girls recently and here are some of their responses:

- "Oh, that donut looks good. Let's go to Krispy Kreme after church!"
- "She is so skinny. I have got to go to the gym."
- "Do you think I would look good in that color red? Maybe if I had a spray tan."

It was incredible to hear what my girls said based on the photos they saw.

Begin group time and ask girls to identify some of the ways the images they saw in the magazine influenced them. How they wanted to look. What they wished they had. Where they wanted to travel. Help them to see that our surroundings, what and who we place in front of our eyes, impacts us.

PRESS PLAY

Watch the Session Four Video (included in the DVD Kit). Allow time for group discussion afterward.

LET'S TALK

In this passage we want girls to compare and contrast the influence Daniel had on those around him with the influence King Nebuchadnezzar had on those around him. It is also a vital time to discuss how we can only influence people in a way that honors Jesus if we are, in fact, honoring Jesus with our lives.

- Help them identify areas in Scripture that show us how people responded to King Nebuchadnezzar. How did they feel about him? How were they treated? How were those people influenced by having him in their life?

- On the other hand, ask girls to identify areas in Scripture that show us how people responded to Daniel. What did they think of him? How did he make them feel? How did he impact them?

- Emphasize that God purposed us to influence people with our lives for the sake of bringing Him glory.

- We are *all* called to be influencers and world changers.

- We are not able to point people to Jesus with our lives if we are not honoring Him in the way we live and love others. Help make this personal for girls. For example: A girl who attends a wild party on a Saturday night and shows up for Sunday school the next morning. What does this communicate to others?

HERE & NOW

Direct girls to draw a circle in their journals or on a piece of paper you provide. In the center of the circle, ask them to write their name. Now ask them to write the names of people who influence them around their own name in the circle. This is their circle of influence. Girls may have trouble making this personal, so you can ask them leading questions such as:

- Whose opinion do you care about the most?
- Who do you seek wisdom from?
- Who do you talk to every day?

Ask them to consider if the people in their circles are positive or negative influences. Are these relationships part of a biblical community or are they unhealthy?

Help girls understand what it looks like to actively work through unhealthy relationships in a kind and loving way.

FOLLOW UP

When we challenge girls to act on what we learn in Scripture, we mean it! Encourage them not to forget the truths God revealed to us in the group time. Ask them to share specific ways they are implementing the truth of Scripture into their lives this week.

Daniel 5

GET STARTED

Truth is a touchy subject. As we get started today, be mindful of girls in your group who may be uncomfortable during this particular subject. I would have been one of them in my student ministry years. Sadly, I was the recipient of many tough truths spoken to me in love because I often chose to lie. Meaning, any lessons like this one would have made me want to run into the bathroom and hide until the end of the group session. My encouragement to you is not to shy away from the truth of this passage, but to dive in with tenderness and grace.

If you have a middle school group, play two truths and a lie! You know the drill. Ask girls to make three statements aloud. Two truths and one that is untrue. Allow the other group members to guess which one is false. At the end of this game allow them an opportunity to share why truth is important to them.

In case you're dying to figure out the false answers in the Amy Byrd Truth Trivia activity, here they are. 2. Amy gets tan in the summer. 1. Amy speaks French. 3. Amy has been skydiving three times.

If you have a high school group, start today and dive in with real talk.

Ask the girls these questions:
- Does our world value the truth?
- Do you value the truth? Why?
- Is the truth hard to hear? Why?

PRESS PLAY

Watch the Session Five Video (included in the DVD Kit). Allow time for group discussion afterward.

LET'S TALK

Daniel was called to speak tough truth.

Our girls are called to speak tough truth. No, not to a king. But if you know girls very well, you know standing up for truth in the middle of a group of sassy teenage girls might as well be speaking tough truth to a king ... a very sassy king. Girls will be faced with honoring the truth or avoiding speaking it in different seasons for the rest of their lives.

Don't miss these key points:
- God gave wisdom and truth to Daniel.
- God called Daniel to speak this truth to an unbelieving king.
- Daniel spoke this truth no matter the circumstances.
- Daniel could not control what the king did with this truth.

Girls will work through this in detail in their homework, but help them to see that God gave Daniel the truth and Daniel's job was to speak it.

This is an incredible opportunity for girls to consider how they might respond if they are called to speak the truth in scary, uncomfortable moments.

HERE & NOW

Challenge the girls in your group to identify at least one person in their life who God is calling them to speak the truth in love to. It may be an unbelieving sibling, someone they sit next to in math, or even a neighbor. Empower them to speak the truth without fear! Ask them to give you the first name of this person so your group can be praying together, or you can just ask girls to identify this person in their minds. Either way, allow some prayer time at the end of your study and pray together as a group for the boldness to be women of God who value truth.

FOLLOW UP

Check in with your girls during the week to see how they are doing. Remind them of the challenge to speak the truth in love to someone this week. Give encouragement to those who need it.

Daniel 6

GET STARTED

This week's lesson, for my heart at least, is so exciting and so overwhelming all at the same time. We will study Daniel's obedience to God and compare that to the way God calls us to be obedient to Him with our lives.

Let's begin our time today looking at the first layer of obedience we ever knew. Rules our parents gave us when we were young. Ask your girls to call out some rules they had as kids.

Here are some that my girls provided:
- Do not touch the stove.
- Do not go outside by yourself.
- Do not climb on the furniture.

Then ask the girls these questions:
- Why did your parents give you these rules?
- Why was it important to be obedient to these rules?

Basically, we want our girls to see how the ones we are called to obey often know best. Our parents were doing what was best for us by giving us rules and guidelines, and we were called to be obedient to them.

God is doing what is best for us in every detail of our lives, in and out of every season, and we are called to be obedient to Him. Even if we do not understand.

PRESS PLAY

Watch the Session Six Video (included in the DVD Kit). Allow time for group discussion afterward.

LET'S TALK

This story is very familiar to so many. Girls have grown up reading picture books of a man in a den of furry, cute lions. Help them to set the stage here. Help them to understand the severity of the situation in this chapter of Daniel. And like Daniel, we are all called to a lifetime of obedience.

- Point out the actions of the men in court. Help girls to understand this as persecution. Provide some current examples of persecution in our world today.

- Walk girls through Daniel's response to this persecution.
    - He could have been angry, lashed out, or sought revenge.
    - Instead he sought, trusted, and obeyed God.

- Take this time to review King Nebuchadnezzar, King Belshazzar, and King Darius. Ask the girls to share about each of them and the spiritual journey God took them on. Help girls in your group connect how God used Daniel's obedience to impact each of them.

- Spend some time discussing the reality of the lions' den and how Daniel was truly sentenced to death.
    - How did Daniel respond to this sentence?

- Ask girls to identify the areas of the passage where we see Daniel's obedience making a mark on King Darius.

HERE & NOW

Share a story from your own life about a season when God called you to obedience in the midst of fear. Your own lions' den. Your vulnerability will spark the same in them. Give them an opportunity to share areas of their lives where God might be calling them to obedience. Encourage them to be honest about why this scares them. End the time with prayer and the surrendering of our fears and doubts in obedience to God.

FOLLOW UP

My prayer for this week is that your girls opened up about where God might be calling them. What an incredible opportunity for you to get an in-depth look at what the Lord is doing in their hearts! Do not let this dialogue end here. Connect with your girls and encourage them to continue to work out the call God has placed on their lives, face their fears, and remind them they are not alone in that call!

Daniel 1-6

GET STARTED

You've made it to the final week of the study!

If I was mean, I would tell you to host a Daniel themed party and only serve vegetables and water. But I think all girls everywhere would revolt. Let's be honest, if there's no queso or sprinkle cookies, they might not show up. Am I right?

This week is a celebration! Of what God did in the life of Daniel. Of what God has done in the life of these girls in studying Daniel.

Start out by letting girls share the main lessons God has taught them over the last six sessions. Give them an opportunity to share—and I would encourage you to share as well. God has been at work and we don't want to miss any opportunity to celebrate that!

PRESS PLAY

Watch the Session Seven Video (included in the DVD Kit). Allow time for group discussion afterward.

LET'S TALK

This week we will ask girls to create their own timeline of faith. The story of God's sovereignty in their lives.

What better way to guide them through their timeline than by leading them through yours? Share your story, even if they have heard it one million times, and help them see the thread of God's sovereignty in your own life.

HERE & NOW

Encourage girls to post their timeline of faith somewhere visible. Somewhere obnoxious. Somewhere they cannot miss! Challenge them not to forget the lessons learned in the pages of Daniel but instead to live a life changed by the truth we've learned.

session seven: sovereign over all

sources

SESSION ONE

1. *CSB Study Bible* (Nashville: B&H Publishing Group, 2017), 1324.

2. *The MacArthur Study Bible* (Nashville: Thomas Nelson, 2015), 1225.

3. Home. *Merriam-Webster* (online), [cited 1 May 2018]. Available from the internet at https://www.merriam-webster.com/dictionary/home

4. Origin. *Merriam-Webster* (online), [cited 1 May 2018]. Available from the internet at https://www.merriam-webster.com/dictionary/origin

5. Defile. *Merriam-Webster* (online), [cited 1 May 2018]. Available from the internet at https://www.merriam-webster.com/dictionary/defile

SESSION TWO

1. Shauna Niequist, *Bittersweet: Thoughts on Change, Grace, and Learning the Hard Way* (Grand Rapids: Zondervan, 2010), 187.

SESSION THREE

1. Bow. *Merriam-Webster* (online), [cited 1 May 2018]. Available from the internet at https://www.merriam-webster.com/dictionary/bow

2. Corrie ten Boom, *The Hiding Place* (Grand Rapids: Chosen Books, 2006), 94.

3. Kenneth O. Gangel, Mywsb.com (online), [cited 1 May 2018]. *Holman Old Testament Commentary: Daniel* (Nashville: Brodman & Holman Publishers, 2001).

SESSION FOUR

1. Mywsb.com (online), [cited 1 May 2018]. *The New American Commentary- Daniel* (Nashville: B&H Publishing Group, 1998).

2. John Piper, Nebuchadnezzar Part 4, *Desiring God* (online), [cited 1 May 2018]. Available from the internet at https://www.desiringgod.org/articles/nebuchadnezzar

SESSION FIVE

1. Strong's H1-'ab, *Blue Letter Bible* (online), [cited 1 May 2018]. Available from the internet at, https://www.blueletterbible.org/lang/lexicon/lexicon.cfm?strongs=H1

2. *ESV: Study Bible* (Wheaton: Crossway Bibles, 2008), 1595.

3. Matt Chandler, *Creature of the Word: The Jesus-Centered Church* (Nashville: B&H Publishing Group, 2012), 176.

SESSION SIX

1. *CSB Apologetics Study Bible* (Nashville: Holman Bible Publishers, 2017), 1053.

2. Sally Lloyd-Jones, *Jesus Storybook Bible: Every Story Whispers His Name* (Grand Rapids: Zondervan, 2007), 152.

STUDY THE FEARLESS WOMEN IN SCRIPTURE
AND THEIR EXTRAORDINARY GOD WITH
BEAUTIFUL ENCOUNTERS AND *A BEAUTIFUL STORY.*

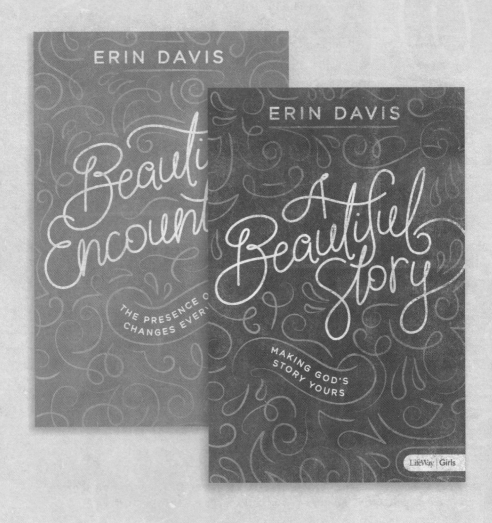

Stories are powerful. From Adam and Eve's catastrophic sin in Eden to the Israelites' dramatic rescue, the stories of God and His people grip us. But even the most memorable Bible story is just the backdrop for an even bigger narrative.

Beautiful Encounters examines eleven New Testament women who were changed by Jesus Christ. *A Beautiful Story* explores the lives of ten Old Testament women. Author Erin Davis taps into the power of story and Old and New Testament truths to help young women understand God's character and redemptive plan in all of Scripture.

PICK UP YOUR COPY AT LIFEWAY.COM/GIRLS OR A LOCAL LIFEWAY CHRISTIAN STORE. QUESTIONS? CALL OUR CUSTOMER SERVICE TEAM AT 800.458.2772.